DATE DUE

GAYLORD			PRINTED IN U.S.A.

The Truth About School Violence

Keeping Healthy Schools Safe

Jared M. Scherz

Rowman & Littlefield Education
Lanham, Maryland • Toronto • Oxford
2006

Published in the United States of America
by Rowman & Littlefield Education
A Division of Rowman & Littlefield Publishers, Inc.
A wholly owned subsidary of The Rowman & Littlefield Publishing
Group, Inc.
4501 Forbes Boulevard, Suite 200, Lanham, Maryland 20706
www.rowmaneducation.com

PO Box 317
Oxford
OX2 9RU, UK

British Library Cataloguing in Publication Information Available

Library of Congress Cataloging-in-Publication Data

Scherz, Jared.
  The truth about school violence : keeping healthy schools safe / Jared
M. Scherz.
      p. cm.
  Includes bibliographical references.
  ISBN-13: 978-1-57886-456-0 (hardcover : alk. paper)
  ISBN-13: 978-1-57886-457-7 (pbk. : alk. paper)
  ISBN-10: 1-57886-456-9 (hardcover : alk. paper)
  ISBN-10: 1-57886-457-7 (pbk. : alk. paper)
  1. School violence—United States—Prevention. I. Title.
  LB3013.32.S32 2006
  371.7'82—dc22

                                              2006002251

To my daughters, Sera and Cassie.
I hope your academic future is
wonderfully rewarding.

Contents

Foreword

Over 30 years ago I decided to focus my dissertation around the issue of organizational health. At the time I was an elementary school principal who had been hired to bring change to an elementary school in an affluent community. As I looked at the change process it occurred to me that before making a change, I needed to create a healthy organization, so I focused on that and wrote about it.

As I worked on the dissertation, I came to understand that health is not the absence of disease, but it is an affirmative state that is created through the provision of a number of positive elements that create a climate of possibility in the organization. I also came to realize how few organizations understand this or attend to it. I believe that is one of the major reasons why change is so difficult and all too rare. Change is the house built upon the foundation of health. Without the foundation, the house will not stand.

Imagine my delight when Jared Scherz shared with me his plans for a book about school violence that would base its actions on the creation of organizational health. I believe that is exactly the way the issue of violence needs to be addressed. Sadly, far too often in our culture, we wait for something to happen and then try to fix it. It is the old "locking the barn door after the horse has escaped" notion that my mother warned me about as a child. We see it over and over. If someone flies planes into buildings, we spend billions, after the fact, on intelligence and airport security to try to prevent it from happening again. With hurricane Katrina, we did not spend millions to strengthen the levees and then had to spend billions to clean up the damage caused by broken levees. We know that inoculations save money as opposed to treatment or that education saves money as opposed to individuals going to prison, but we invest on the wrong end of the process.

Columbine, Red Lake, Paducah, and so many others have become education's Twin Towers and broken levees. The issue of school violence has caused many to fix the back end of the process and to ignore the front end. So many schools opted for metal detectors and school resource officers as a solution to violence, when the real solution would be found in prevention.

Education is about relationships—the relationship of children to learning, but also the relationship of children to other children and the relationship of adults to children. If those relationships have not been nurtured, then it is difficult to expect good things to happen.

The creation of organizational health is a journey toward wholeness. All aspects of the organization must be aligned and considered. That is really what this book is about—a search for wholeness. Jared Scherz understands that you can't fix one thing, you must heal everything. So much of the school reform literature assumes that education is a mechanistic process that can be fixed by pulling separate parts out, tuning them up, and moving on. Education, since it is above all a human enterprise, is an organic process where all the elements must be considered. As stated in this book, "violence is not simply the problem; it is the result of many problems gone unanswered." The search for organizational health is an attempt to deal with those "many problems" particularly in a preventive way.

It also strikes me that the issue of violence in schools is really an issue of power—who has it and who doesn't. Sadly, in today's context, neither the children nor the adults working within the system tend to have a lot of power. Often, the creation of violence is an attempt to grab that missing power. A major part of the solution must be to address the issue of power and the relationships of individuals to it so that healthy and appropriate responses are available. One of the major ingredients in health is the creation of adaptability—that is, at its core, an attempt to create a sense of personal power. It addresses issues such as resiliency. I believe that the creation of resiliency in children, adults, or even societies is the quickest path away from their resorting to violence as an answer to their sense of powerlessness.

Jared Scherz addresses this issue of adaptability but he also addresses two other pillars of organizational health—climate and infrastructure. Most school folks understand infrastructure well—they manage it daily. They need to understand that all pieces must be addressed in regard to violence prevention. It is not enough to have metal detectors if you don't have good policies on bullying and harassment. It is not enough to have clear sightlines in halls if the building feels like a prison.

This leads to the creation of climate. Climate is one of those things that is hard to describe but easy to spot. You know it when you see it. It shows up in the smiles on faces, the familiarity of the principal to the children, and in a thousand other small, but significant ways. And if it is bad, you have the potential for big problems.

Finding the "Whole Truth" about school violence is coming to understand that everything in education is connected to everything else and that getting a handle on creating a healthful learning environment is the surest way to prevent something terrible from happening. And that would be a good change.

Paul D. Houston
Executive Director
American Association of School Administrators

Acknowledgments

There are many people who helped this book come to fruition. All of their ideas, insights, encouragement, and willingness to address this challenging topic are truly appreciated.

Special appreciation goes to educational consultant Eileen Murphy for her creative collaboration over the past 5 years. Her expertise in turning ideology into pragmatics was tremendously valuable. Research for this book was made possible by educators across the country, including many principals from the NAESP and schools in New York and New Jersey. Their recognition of the need for educational research, their time, and their energy are deeply appreciated. I thank Drs. Theopia Jackson, Royal Alsup (Liberation Pyschology), and Susan Campbell for their philosophical and ideological support. I also thank Sherri Martin for her help with providing clarity and lucidity to the academic work that laid the foundation for this book. Thank you Robert for your ongoing help with research and analysis of the data.

And finally to my wife, Donna, who provided infinite encouragement and ceaseless sacrifice, without which I would not have found the time or energy to complete this project.

Introduction

A 17-year-old male student in a southeast Washington, D.C., high school died on February 2, 2004, after being shot several times in the chest around 10:30 A.M. near the school's cafeteria. The shooter was a fellow student who said he panicked after he was shot in the leg, so he pulled out his gun and started firing. It was later discovered that he shot himself in the leg while pulling his gun out of his pants.

On February 3, 2004, in the bathroom of their school, a 14-year-old Florida teenager was cut across his throat by a boy who was said to be his best friend. The perpetrator kept a journal with tips on how to become a serial killer.

On March 17, 2004, a seventh grader in Joyce, Washington, committed suicide in his language arts class in the presence of his classmates using a rifle he had brought in a guitar case.

In Pharr, Texas, on March 29, 2004, a 15-year-old female student was stabbed to death by a fellow classmate while they waited for rides home following a dramatic arts competition. The custodian witnessed the stabbing but thought the students were acting out a scene from the competition.

In Red Lake, Minnesota, on March 21, 2005, a teen shot nine people dead and injured seven others. It was the worst tragedy since the Columbine incident over five years prior.

In 2002, students between the ages of 12 and 18 were victims of about 309,000 serious violent crimes away from school, compared with about 88,000 occurring at school. Many of the incidents off school grounds stemmed from unresolved conflicts at school, such as bullying, dating troubles, and retaliation.

The self-proclaimed experts on student violence tell us we should do a better job predicting who the "at-risk" students are. The media often focus on the need for better bullying prevention and character development programs. Schools seek to create weapon-free environments. While these may be aspects of reducing the potential for violence in our nation's schools, they only address a small fraction of the issues.

The week after the stabbing in Pharr, Texas, school authorities met to discuss weapons searches for students and athletes who were on grounds for extracurricular activities. Although this may prevent another stabbing on school property, it does not address the complex roots for violent behavior—it simply forces a change in venue for the violent act. Schools, communities, and families must work together to help students resolve conflicts in a nonviolent manner rather than continue to espouse the "it won't happen here" philosophy.

There is growing evidence to support the premise that school culture affects the level of violence among students—both on and off campus—but there is insufficient data connecting the effect of the social system of schools on student violence.

What does school culture look like? When we think of successful schools we can imagine teachers who can connect with students, parents who take an active role, students who are eager to learn, and administrators who create an atmosphere of support and encouragement, which permeates throughout the building. Change any of these aspects and the culture of the school changes.

What happens when the school staff feels fragmented and hopeless? What happens when the students are apathetic? When the parents are uninvolved? When the administrators are or feel ineffective?

A number of other authors have looked at school "climate" and "culture," although we are still learning how educators' perceptions of these factors influence prevention efforts. What we do know is that there aren't good or bad school cultures, but instead there are assets and limitations, which, like a person, can be measured.

School culture is best measured by the organizational health of the institution. Although organizational health is not a new concept in organizational development literature, the relationship with school violence has not yet been clearly defined. In this book, organizational health will be broken down into three practical dimensions that can be targeted for improvement in your school system:

Adaptation: This includes important areas such as resiliency, organizational awareness, and school learning. Five specific factors that allow a school to keep pace with the internal and external pressures forcing change are discussed.

Climate: It is important to appreciate the importance of the mood, milieu, and temperament of your school, which affects your relationships with colleagues, students, and others in the administrative hierarchy of schools. It is also important to review the role of leadership in creating a safe school environment.

Infrastructure: This includes the tangible aspects of your school culture, such as the physical environment, policies, procedures, vision, and mission statement, to determine their efficacy.

It is not simply these three dimensions but their interaction that forms the basis of organizational health. This book will provide educators, school board members, politicians, and parents with a detailed outline of the important components of organizational health. If these components are consistently addressed, the school's health will improve and ultimately the potential for violence will be reduced.

GOALS OF THIS BOOK

The past decade has repeatedly shown that student violence does not discriminate against any school regardless of wealth, location, size, or resources. It is a naive educator who says "it could never happen here." This head-in-the-sand approach can end in a posttragedy reflection, with the educator wondering what could have been done differently. The educator for whom prevention and continuous improvement of organizational health is an aspect of day-to-day planning will be rewarded by a cohesive school environment, free from violence. This educator will also avoid the horror and self-recrimination of posttragedy reflection.

Prevention is often overlooked in educational systems because financial and human resources are already spread thin, keeping up with the increasing demands of contemporary education. Each community has unique budgetary and personnel challenges, and, therefore, a uniform solution for all schools is not appropriate. In this book you will be given strategies on creating the best approach for your school, balancing content with process.

Existing violence prevention programs will be discussed with this focus in mind, recognizing successful planning includes a combination of what to do and how to do it. As an example, antibullying curriculum can be theoretically very sound, but if the skills taught are not appreciated and utilized by the students, the program will not be successful. It is crucial to continually monitor the effectiveness of the delivery methods and review the receptivity of the students.

How will this book help? Educators, parents, and others invested in the academic and social success of our children who fully understand the nature of student violence will do a better job of reducing its potential. As I suggested in my first book, *Harnessing the Power of Resistance: A Guide for Educators*, an artful educator can learn to harness the energy of the workplace for positive results.

My goal in this book is to raise your awareness of your school's organizational health. Healthy schools continually improve every aspect of the working and learning environment. This leads to the important by-product of reduced potential for violence.

Beyond discussing the three dimensions of organizational health, the practical and specific definitions will provide opportunities to create blueprints for transforming your own school's culture. The first step is providing a common language and shared understanding among educators, making the process of collaborating with others easier.

This book is meant to be a transformative tool. Whether your school needs major reform or strengthening of already effective systems, you will find sound strategies in the following pages. This is not a "how-to" book that gives repeated suggestions for making changes in your school but more of a provocative tool to expand your perspective, challenge your current beliefs, and lastly to provide a framework from which improvements can be made.

Part I

ETIOLOGY OF VIOLENCE

CHAPTER 1

Defining the Issue

As evidenced on September 11, 2001, violence is far-reaching and irreversibly destructive. The decision to act violently can alter the life of a person, a school system, a community, and even a planet, as we have seen over the course of the past decade. Whether the decision of a lone gunman, fixed on political assassination, or the elaborate plans of a couple of students who feel ostracized by their peers, violent solutions to problems can irrevocably alter the course of history.

Our students see violence espoused as a justified means to solving a problem by world leaders who turn to acts of war as responses for a broad spectrum of real or perceived offenses—from genocide to economic pressures.

Throughout this book you will find both an expansive and a detailed examination of a concept that has become increasingly complicated over the course of time. What we referred to as violent 50 years ago is not an accurate reflection in today's society. Due to our varied background and experiences, it makes sense that we define violence differently. For the purpose of this book, we will offer a definition used by the Center for Substance Abuse Prevention, an organization that specializes in this field, and then we will move on to broaden the focus and make it more applicable to school systems: "Violence includes any emotional, psychological, or physical harm to person, community, or property. Violence is not isolated to any one community or segment of the population; rather it is multidimensional and pervasive."

TYPES OF VIOLENCE

The multidimensionality of violence is reflected in the various forms of aggression found throughout the world. Ethnic cleansing is a quasireligiously motivated form of genocide intended to eradicate an entire culture. Date rape is a form of social violence perpetrated mainly by younger males for the purposes of dominance and sexual gratification. Child abuse is often discussed alongside domestic violence and is viewed as interpersonal oppression to gain power and control. While these terms conjure up certain images few would dispute, not everybody in the world will agree what defines violence.

What we define as violence may be debated based on certain moral, cultural, and religious standards. The genital mutilation of 6,000 girls a day or 200,000 girls annually across the world is viewed by many as traditional tribal custom. The sacrifice of certain animals is protected as a right in many countries for religious observation. On a regional level, certain forms of disciplining children with physical force is customary.

Other types of violence within other subsets of our population provide further evidence of this country's proclivity toward aggression. In the United States, one in five women will be a victim of rape in her lifetime, with approximately 248,000 rape cases reported in 2002 (Rennison & Rand, 2003). Sexual assault and harassment are not limited to adults; in fact, the more extreme cases of assault begin with lower levels of violence among school-aged children. In one study of 1,600 youth of mixed ethnicity, 85% of girls and 76% of boys reported experiencing some form of sexual harassment in school (Dupper & Meyer-Adams, 2002). It is at these early ages that the tone is set for acceptable and nonacceptable sexualized interaction of peers.

The victimization of presumed gays and lesbians is another form of violence; in fact, it is the most common form of bias-related violence in the United States. Hate crimes at school extend beyond verbal harassment, as reports indicate approximately 25% of males and females indicate being physically hurt by other students because of their sexual orientation.

The threat of violence has similar psychological effects as violence itself, as indicated by research on child maltreatment. Do we group the *threat* of violence as intimidation, thus falling under the category of emotional abuse, or do we separate it into its own category?

There are many questions about how to distinguish, differentiate, and ultimately understand better the nature of violence and the efficacy of prevention. The most logical place to begin this understanding is at its earliest stage of development.

Youth Violence

There is little debate that youth violence is a national epidemic worthy of considerable attention. Youth violence, as its counterpart with adults, is complex in its manifestation and so too are our prevention and intervention efforts. If we are dealing with drug-related violence by inner-city youth, for instance, we may focus more attention on community activities and other social outlets to dissuade gang involvement. How we intervene in this situation will be significantly different from how we would address sexual harassment in a middle or upper socioeconomic community.

In the 10 years from 1983 to 1993, arrests of youth charged with serious violent offenses surged by 70% (Shalala, 1994). In those same years the number of young people who committed homicides tripled. In the past decade, according to the National Secretary for Health and Human Services, there has been a gradual steadying of youth violence, less prevalent than in the previous 10 years though it still remains among the most threatening epidemics facing this country. Violence ranks among the five leading causes of death for those under 24 years old and the second leading cause of death for African American males aged 15 to 19 (Shalala, 1994). Fifteen children die as a result of gunfire every day in this country. That is almost 5,500 child deaths a year, by guns alone (Shalala, 1994). In 1997, of teens under the age of 18 years, 1,700 were implicated in 1,400 murders (Snyer, 2002).

The Centers for Disease Control and Prevention (as cited in Havemann, 1997) reports the United States has the highest rates of childhood homicide, suicide, and firearms-related deaths of any of the world's 26 richest nations. This is not a recent trend, as a 1991 study found that the United States had homicide rates among youth that were eight times higher than the rates of other industrialized countries (Hampton, Jenkins, & Gullotta, 1996). Similar comparisons hold for youth suicide as well, with the United States reporting twice that of other industrialized nations for children under 14.

When attempting to understand the causes for youth violence it is important to examine the sequence of events that lead to aggression. An important distinction not yet distinguished by researchers within the area of youth violence is whether violence is initiated or a response to stimuli.

While national surveys done by government agencies and private industry regarding statistics of school violence show evidence of perpetrators committing aggressive acts, few studies make the distinction whether violence is retaliatory for other forms of harassment. Retaliatory violence has captured news headlines in recent years because of its catastrophic and demonstrative nature. In situations such as Columbine, Little Rock, and Jonesboro, students who committed these vicious acts were seeking revenge for real and perceived abuse they had endured throughout years of schooling.

Retaliatory Violence

Retaliatory violence is not an act of aggression that stems from the unmet basic needs of food or shelter, such as in the case of many poverty stricken inner-city schools, but instead is more about affiliation and belonging. The bottom line for retaliatory violence is a desperate response, incubated in a school community that has failed to recognize the tremendous pain of less resilient youth from middle- and upper-class strata.

Schools have struggled with their culpability to manage the behavior of students both on and off their property. Understandably challenging for districts that struggle to improve test scores and even increase student attendance is the issue of aggression. Despite the obstacles, schools may be viewed as taking less responsibility for their social environment, leaving children to resolve problems on their own, or at least off of school property.

The problem with a hands-off mentality in today's world is the way in which children attempt to deal with matters of rejection and disrespect. This problem is more likely than ever to end in catastrophe, often permeating the boundaries of the school. Gone are the days of one-on-one fisticuffs to settle disputes, now replaced by use of automatic weapons and homemade explosives, which students are not afraid to infiltrate the once-safe confines of the school building.

Dramatic Violence

If many categories of school violence are not escalating, and the overall threat of violence in schools may not be increasing, why is the perception of the threat of violence in schools so strong? Perhaps the severity of violence among this country's students plays a role in public perception. A review of well-publicized near catastrophic and catastrophic events in our nation's schools from the past decade may illustrate this point.

Overall, the rate of multiple homicides shows one of the few increases in school violence. In the 6 years from July 1992 to December 1998, there were 13 school shootings involving multiple victims in the United States (Williams, 1998). In the 2 years *not including* but following the Columbine tragedy (up to 2003), there were 7 incidents in separate schools, in which 23 people were wounded and 6 were killed (Bower, 2001). Eleven more near catastrophes were averted, such as the plot in Port Huron, Michigan, in May 1999, in which two young students were caught with a list of 154 targets, a stolen building plan, and a previously confiscated handgun. In February 2001, an 18-year-old in Elmira, New York, was apprehended with a handgun, a duffel bag containing 18 bombs, and a sawed-off shotgun.

These were only two of the widely publicized incidents that influence public perception. While there is no evidence to support the notion that overall trends in violence are increasing, there is a rise in the randomness and severity of violent episodes. The younger age of perpetrators along with the rise in dramatic violence lead us to consider how young people are being influenced toward this overtly antisocial behavior and what may be reinforcing their behavior.

CONTAGION OF VIOLENCE

Youth who witness chronic and catastrophic violence as part of their daily lives will not be influenced with simple educational programs. As an example, consider the first- and second-grade students in Washington, D.C., who were surveyed by the American Psychological Association (1993). Of these students 45% had witnessed muggings, 31% had witnessed shootings, and 39% had seen a dead body. These youngsters have already begun to form strong opinions on violence based on their personal experiences. Violence is often viewed as an acceptable form of problem solving in communities where being "soft" can be an exploited weakness. A violence prevention program for them must take their social reality into account.

The spread of violence across the age spectrum and the severity of incidents we have witnessed throughout the country suggest that youth are learning to resolve conflicts by watching each other. The *contagion of violence* is a term that is sometimes referred to in the media as the Columbine Effect. This phenomenon is well documented in social psychology literature, being studied around youth suicide in particular. For adolescents who are interested in attracting public awareness to their desperate plight, acts of violence have proven to be an effective tool.

The rise in "copy cat" dramatic violence has certainly heightened the awareness of the general public, perhaps highlighting a new issue. Regardless of whether violence is on the rise in America's schools, the choice for dramatic escalation of problem solving by students in this country appears to be different than in past decades. As a community of social scientists, we seem to be in our infancy of understanding this latest surge of catastrophic violence perpetrated by our students in one school after another. If we begin to explore the causative or contributory factors, we may then be able to develop more effective prevention and intervention strategies.

For the purpose of creating healthy school culture, let us use this broad definition of violence: *an overt or subtle act of aggression, physical harm, intimidation, or coercion resulting in emotional or physical suffering of another.* Based on a common definition, we can create concrete measurements of the value and scope of a prevention program. As we continue to explore the causative and/or contributory factors of systemic, multivariant forms of violence, we will be better equipped to create a more comprhensive prevention philosophy. This new mindset will include optimal strategies for violence reduction born out of the unique cultures of each school, all of which breeds more peaceful conflict resolution.

CHAPTER 2

Schools of Thought

Talking about theory among educators may seem like a misuse of time when immediate solutions for problems like violence are needed; however, a successful long-term approach to prevention makes it imperative. In order to stimulate thinking about existing prevention approaches, we will consider various viewpoints as they relate to particular episodes of violence within a school.

On March 7, 2005, a young Caucasian American male from a suburban middle school in Washington, D.C., was arrested for terroristic threats toward his teacher. This young man, from an upper-middle-class family, was involved in an after-school activity and had a large group of acquaintances, with a couple of close friends. He had no significant history of violence in his family and was not a victim of abuse himself. In fact his parents were happily married with no financial pressure. So what caused this young man to tell his teacher he was going to "put explosives in his car"?

A brief history of events leading up to this arrest reveals a child who had been "acting up" in class, according to his teacher. The teacher sent him to the dean, calling him an interruption to the classroom. The student was sent back to the classroom by the dean with a warning. This pattern repeated itself several times throughout the week with growing frustration from the teacher, who felt unsupported and resentment toward the dean who believed this student should be dealt with in the classroom.

Finally, out of frustration, the teacher said something that embarrassed the student, resulting in social ostracism and ridicule from the boy's peers. Several days later the student made the threat.

In the case that was just presented to you, we could likely take 10 different social scientists and find an equal number of corresponding explanations for what caused him to act aggressively. Let us consider some of these perspectives to determine how their theories hold up.

It is first necessary to conceptualize what causes violence before we can appreciate what causes violence or effectively develop prevention strategies. As with any social phenomenon, violence has been studied from several perspectives, yielding different paradigms.

Researchers from many disciplines attempting to pinpoint the causative factors of violence among youth are responsible for these theories. The majority of their work focuses on early warning signs and individualistic predictors for violence.

The media reinforce the idea of needing improved prediction, which may buttress this narrow approach at prevention. Educators, they say, must do a better job of detecting signs of potential violence in students.

Most theoretical perspectives focus exclusively on the individual who perpetrates the aggression. Violence, from this standpoint, considers the impact of social, familial, and cultural influences, but only as secondary determinants. One such orientation is known as the developmental theory of violence, which considers the intrapsychic process as well as physiological and psychological factors. Issues such as maternal drug and alcohol use, childhood abuse, poverty, and early attachment to a significant caretaker are critical to the healthy or unhealthy development of children. While this theory recognizes that the aforementioned variables impact one's ability to cope with the environment, it does not fully consider familial, cultural, or societal influences, especially as they impact one's propensity to engage in violence.

Developmental theorists propose that traumatized babies and children are at risk of the impairment of necessary capabilities to relate successfully to others. This trauma may influence the proclivity for perpetuating violence.

The developmental theory of violence also includes moral development. Some theorists suggest that a child who is progressing through age-appropriate stages of moral and social development is considered psychologically healthy. Children who behave violently are thought to have delayed, faulty, or incomplete moral development.

So how does our middle school student measure according to the developmental perspective? We could argue that his immaturity and lack of appropriate social skills played a role. After all, if he hadn't been clowning around in class, he never would have been singled out by the teacher, so he wouldn't have been embarrassed. However, we could also argue that another student who experienced the same circumstances may not resort to the same coping mechanism. We might also wonder what role the faculty played in not recognizing the unmet needs of this student or how their lack of synchronicity (dean and teacher) affected the teacher's impatience.

Another well-studied phenomenon in the field of youth violence is the concept of resilience: a measure of the internal capacity of an individual to tolerate duress. How a person responds to stress when his or her capacity for adapting becomes overwhelmed has been studied since the early 1960s.

The notion that youth become unable to cope with their ordinary compensatory mechanisms is important in understanding a large percentage of the retaliatory violence, especially those catastrophic events in the past decade. The inability to cope with one's environment may result in feelings of helplessness. Learned helplessness may result when children are faced with repeated uncontrollable events and do not have the means to deal with the feelings or thoughts that result from these events. Youth who continue to feel victimized or helpless, without any hope for the future, may resort to impulsive acts of aggression. We are also witnessing more calculated acts of violence, suggesting there may be a deeper cause than a lack of resiliency.

It is clear that the student described above had a breakdown in his internal resources to cope with the perceived threat by his teacher.

We might say that he lacked resiliency. Those who are less resilient are likely to feel powerless, making them more susceptible to desperate acts such as violence. As with the previous theoretical paradigm, resiliency is a concept narrow in scope. While it is likely a critical element in any equation that results in violence, it is only one ingredient.

Some criminologists suggest that the explosion of youth crime reflects a growing percentage of children who are unsupervised or otherwise at risk. This is often attributed to the low level of funding associated with social programs in this country. While handgun control groups blame much of the problem on the presence of more than 200 million handguns in American households, racism, poverty, and unequal opportunities are also cited as factors for youth violence prevalent throughout the country.

Apparently, the threat of violence does not fit into any belief system that offers the availability of weapons as a cause. In the situation mentioned above, the young man had not come from a family in which he was unsupervised or lacked resources.

Another school of thought believes students who experience more relational problems may be more inclined to resort to violence. They believe the interpersonal dysfunction stems from students being ostracized and categorized as less than human. Violent retaliation is the student's way of claiming superiority.

Dysfunction within the family system, as a contributing variable to violence, is another school of thought. Family systems theory recognizes that a child's behavior is impacted by the relationships he or she has with family members as well as by the relationships his or her family members have with each other. Children who "act out" are doing so to express a problem for the entire family system.

While the student in the above example could have experienced ongoing relational problems, hence the cause for his attention seeking, he did not have obvious or specific family dysfunction. Even if there were significant familial influences underlying this child's hostility, how does that separate him from the millions of other students with similar or even worse dynamics at home? Deans are charged with protecting the security of their schools and, as such, tend to view discipline problems with a more punitive lens. That is, they address behavior without a full appreciation for the underlying psychological or familial issues at play.

The social ecology of school systems has only recently been explored but without sufficient attention by school administrators. One possible reason for this gap in research pertaining to the school context stems from the fact that within psychology and education, violence is often conceptualized as a behavior associated with cognitive or behavioral deficit.

Another theory suggests that high levels of violence are found in schools in which students feel alienated, and so they become aggressive. Alienation may be in the form of a lack of connectedness to or significant knowledge of other students, teachers, and the school's structure and environment in general. Teachers and children should have the opportunity to interact in a caring and respectful atmosphere in which the best qualities of the child would be developed and the whole child considered for the success of the educational process.

Social alienation is a subcomponent of most relational theories. In many cases of violence, particularly in upper-middle-class suburban schools, there has been has some component of isolation or ostracism. Two of the most famous examples are found in the Columbine massacre. Both students are suspected of feeling on the outside looking in with regard to their social community. With the example given above there also appears to be a component of isolation. While this experience has the potential for creating serious psychological distress, the pervasiveness of alienation is too common and widespread to be the sole component of violence. Nonetheless, we can be mindful of how the school system can address this issue as both an antagonist and a protagonist.

Please keep in mind our working definition of violence: *An overt or subtle act of aggression, physical harm, intimidation, or coercion resulting in emotional or physical suffering of another.*

We might be unable to answer with exact precision why any episode of violence occurs, largely because all theories hold some component of this complex equation. As educators, we can become aware of our tendency to focus on external influences, or those unrelated to the school environment, because they abdicate schools in their responsibility (or reduce the chances of being blamed). To become better students of human (child) behavior, we may seek to understand all theories, in particular the most overlooked ones: the systemic and contextual influences that directly impact the degree of organizational health of schools.

CHAPTER 3

Violence in Schools

HISTORY OF SCHOOL VIOLENCE

Violence within schools became an important issue in the latter half of the 21st century. Prior to the 1950s there was little concern by school administrators with regard to student violence, as evidenced by the fact there is only one known study that exists on the topic—a 1949 survey of high school principals, which found no difficulty with either student violence or destruction of property. In 1956 the National Educational Association (NEA) asserted that violence was becoming more of a concern within the schools (Warner, Weist, & Krulak, 1999).

Cultural, racial, and political issues may have all been factors in the growth of school violence in the 1960s and 1970s. As students were integrated in the 1960s, racial violence (physical and emotional) became a notable issue. The reports of this violence seemed to be limited to urban and rural schools, and this aggression was not considered a pervasive problem. Many believed it would "settle down" as the students became more acclimated to the changes (Warner, Weist, & Krulak, 1999). It is not clear what role the school played in helping both new and existing students adapt to the profound changes they were experiencing.

The early 1970s witnessed the first comprehensive study of school crime, conducted by the National Institute of Education. The conclusion of the study found that adolescents were at greater risk of becoming victims of violence while at school than when away from school. Even with these results, researchers were aware of the substantial underreporting of offenses that masked the seriousness of this national problem (Warner, Weist, & Krulak, 1999).

Congress began to investigate the growing problem of school violence. The House of Representatives held hearings and debated the passage of the Safe Schools Act in 1971, but no action was taken. Despite ongoing discussion it wasn't until 1977 that Congress requested the U.S. Department of Health, Education, and Welfare (HEW) conduct a study on school crime. The HEW department reported that crime was a major issue in 8% of the public schools, leading to recommendations for increased security and for principals to act as disciplinarians (Warner, Weist, & Krulak, 1999).

Few comprehensive studies were conducted in the 1980s, although many smaller scale studies were done. Results from these studies yielded confusing findings for the lawmakers of the time. Although some touted the leveling off in the frequency of violent crime in the late 1970s and early 1980s, the numbers reported were high. A study in the late 1980s, for instance, found that 91,000 teachers—almost 4%—had been attacked physically in that year (Gaustad, 1991).

The numbers for students were even worse. Violence against students in that same year found 34% of those eighth and tenth graders surveyed reported that they had been robbed, threatened, or attacked while at school or on a school bus. It is interesting to compare these numbers with statistics that show that in the same timeframe between 3 and 6% of school teachers are being physically attacked by a student, although it is now from rural, suburban, and urban schools (Greenbaum, 1989).

With these findings, the debate began to shift toward whether students could concentrate on learning when their most basic need for safety and security is compromised. It was also asked how educators could effectively teach under the threat of violence. These questions may have spurred one of the first references to school climate, found in the Safe School Study conducted by the National Institute of Education (NIE) (Warner, Weist, & Krulak, 1999). The study looked at the school environment, in particular the physical layout of the buildings. Risk factors associated with the physical and social structure of the schools were identified.

This may sound inconsequential to those who don't favor history references; however, it is important to recognize how and why the focus expanded to incorporate the school "environment" as a component of violence. With appreciation growing for the magnitude of school violence, in particular in rural and suburban school systems, there was likely an escalating pressure on lawmakers to find answers to this problem. As typically happens when problems become publicized, fingers are pointed in all directions to externalize blame. While it was important to consider the role of the school itself in student violence, this expanded focus did not lead to changes in organizational health, in fact it led to much the opposite.

Studies have continued regarding the nature and etiology of student violence, but the tone of many shifted to one of less immediacy until the Columbine shootings.

CURRENT TRENDS IN STUDENT VIOLENCE

Student violence, a term that is sometimes used to refer to youth violence taking place on school property, is among the most significant threats to public education of our time. The National Center for Educational Statistics reports that in 1999, students aged 12 through 18 were victims of approximately 2.5 million total crimes at school, with about 186,000 of those crimes being serious and violent in nature. Of these violent crimes, 47 school-associated deaths were reported between July 1, 1998, and June 30, 1999, including 38 homicides, 33 of which involved school-aged children (DeVoe et al., 2004).

Violence, once thought of as a social problem in "bad neighborhoods," is now recognized as a national epidemic within all urban, suburban, and rural schools. According to Richard W. Riley, the former secretary of education, there are approximately 16,000 antisocial incidents each school day, or about 1 incident every 6 seconds. The Centers for Disease Control and Prevention reported that in 1999, almost 5% of students (1 in 20) reported carrying a firearm at least once in the previous 30 days (Kaufman, Chen, Choy, Ruddy, & Miller, 2001).

Despite a belief held by some that school violence is limited to urban areas, the most recent school statistics show an equal vulnerability of suburban students (Srebalus, Schwartz, Vaughan, & Tunick, 1996). One study (Sandhu, 2000) found that 6% of the adolescents surveyed in rural states across the country indicated they had at some time brought a gun to school; of this same sample, 42% indicated they had access to a gun if interested. Violence and the threat of violence has certainly penetrated the sanctuaries of suburban schools as well, with approximately 160,000 students across the country missing class each day due to fear of violence at school (DeVoe et al., 2004).

Students and teachers alike are reporting an increased threat of daily violence within their schools. When students feel unsafe, they may experience social, emotional, and learning difficulties. When teachers feel unsafe, they may become unwilling to extend themselves in a way necessary to fully reach their students. With the diversity of threats to our academic integrity, including drugs, gangs, violence, bullying, depression, and countless other issues, students' potential for learning is significantly compromised.

Educators are well aware of the problem, ranking aggression as the number one concern facing our schools and communities.

Prior to September 11, 2001, the media were zoning in on widespread student violence, which raised our collective awareness of the problem. With the recent world events, we await an unknown impact on domestic problems such as youth violence. An argument may be made that our country has become more unified through trauma and thus the level of youth violence has declined. On the contrary, however, trauma often gives rise to increased energy toward self-preservation, which may in the long term exaggerate the problem.

What we do know at this point is that the level of dramatic and retaliatory violence, sometimes referred to as catastrophic violence, is on the rise. One only need to look at a recent magazine or watch a news report to appreciate the frequency and intensity with which tragic or near tragic events are taking place. Whether it be on a school bus or in a cafeteria, the schools have become breeding grounds for bold statements of hopelessness from our students. We need to become more curious about this recent trend and begin to speculate as to why catastrophic violence is rising.

The immediate but unpopular answer is that our changing culture has found schools to be more vulnerable than ever before. Many schools are ill equipped to address the complexity of student violence and in many cases have become catalysts for explosiveness. For those schools that are unaware of their role in perpetuating this problem act as self-contained pressure cookers that breed the dramatic violence we are now witnessing.

There has also been a change in the nature of aggression within schools. More violent episodes involving the use of weapons are reported than ever before. California is one of the few states that mandate the maintenance of statistics regarding violence in schools. The California Department of Education (1990) reported a 28% overall rise in the use of weapons, with a 100% increase in gun-related incidents during the 1980s. This statistic was further broken down into a 50% increase in elementary schools, a 79% increase in middle schools, and a 142% increase at the high school level for weapon possession. At the same time in Florida, a 42% increase in gun-related incidents was reported (Gaustad, 1991). It is evident that not only is school violence restricted by geographic regions, it is also not isolated to particular communities or socioeconomic status.

Many reports show that statistically youth violence is at a constant level overall. Specific categories, such as female student violence, are on the rise, but male violence has declined. for instance. Because these reports are based on a broad variety of definitions of violence, comparing one to the other is simply confusing the issues. We also know that underreporting exists because victims are afraid of being further victimized, while schools are fearful of being stigmatized as violent.

To get a good sense of what is happening in our schools, we can examine the perception of safety for the teachers and the students. A Met Life survey (Markow, Fauth, & Gravitch, 2002) found students are more likely to report feeling "very safe" at school than they had been in the previous 5 years. Despite this, another study stated 25% of high school students fear violence in schools. Are we comparing similar issues? Do students who report fearing violence at school feel that it will not happen to them, therefore, they report feeling personally safe? Is a student who says he feels safe really reporting that he does not fear harassment, bullying, or undue pressures?

So far we have looked at the history and trends of violence, the various theoretical perspectives around causes of violence, and the discrepancy between perceptions and statistics. As we continue to build our picture of school violence and our philosophy of prevention, we need to explore the inner workings of the school system and the hidden influences of the various dimensions of organizational health. Perhaps the most important of the unanswered questions are what role does the school play and what can the school do to help?

Part II

ORGANIZATIONAL DYNAMICS

CHAPTER 4

Health

In the previous section we defined violence, compared past and current trends, and examined different perspectives regarding the causes of this national epidemic. In the upcoming chapters we are going to broaden our perspective regarding the causes of student aggression by exploring certain contextual influences of the school as an institution.

Large companies have spent billions of dollars on organizational psychologists and consultants to help them understand and improve productivity. In large part this work is focused on the organizational dynamics that directly impact employee behavior. Schools, however, are not nearly as affluent as these companies, so securing this valuable resource is more challenging. Our focus, then, will be to help supplement the lack of professional resources available to schools by addressing the important dimensions of school culture. Ultimately the goal is to gain a greater awareness of the components that make up a healthy school, the likes of which can reduce the potential for student aggression.

While the concept of organizational health has been addressed in books and articles, there does not appear to be much literature addressing the uniqueness of organizational health as it applies to school systems. Many authors address aspects of school culture, but do not address the larger issue of organizational health within the educational system.

For example, Jane Bluestein (2001), in addressing school dynamics, writes about a school's personality. She describes this concept as the school's physical layout combined with the attitudes, interactions, and behaviors of the people. Peterson and Deal (1998) explain a phenomenon called "toxic culture," which they use to characterize schools with staff fragmentation, negative values, and hopelessness, and the mistaken goal of serving adults over students. These authors, along with numerous others, have advanced our recognition of school culture; however, there may be some confusion about the terminology being used.

While organizational culture and health are overlapping yet distinct concepts, it is important to distinguish the two. Culture has received substantial attention, yet organizational health has received insufficient attention in both the organizational development and educational reform literature. Perhaps it wasn't as important in the past to apply the concept of organizational health to the educational system, as schools were small and less complex. Currently, however, the health of a school system may be directly linked to a number of important concerns such as student violence, but also issues such as faculty turnover rates and a growing financial crisis. These problems did not exist to the same degree or at least have not received the same attention they do in this new millennium.

As the American educational system becomes increasingly bureaucratic, school leaders are forced to act more as CEOs. With this change, organizational theory becomes more applicable to the school system. Production is a measurement term previously associated with businesses and not with the social-service delivery systems; however, it has important meaning for educators. As we take a look at productivity, which in school systems can be test scores, graduation rates, or even absenteeism, we can be mindful of one danger—the risk of buttressing the current movement in American politics toward standardization.

While it is necessary to establish benchmarks of success for student education, we can be careful not to dehumanize the workplace of educators by using test scores as the sole indicator of a school's success. Instead, it would behoove us to consider first and foremost the quality of the work and learning environment, which will hereafter be encompassed by the term *organizational health*.

Measuring success in schools remains an important question, even if it is not the sole indicator for school health. If we do not know to what degree schools are accomplishing their primary goal of educating children, then we cannot make informed choices to improve this work. A sensible place to begin this inquiry is the mission and vision statements—the documents that are intended to represent the goal of schools. For most schools this document once created is never heard or seen again. In fact the majority of faculty may have difficulty reciting any part of it, much less use it as a guiding influence in decision making. For those schools at the forefront of contemporary education, there may be more emphasis placed on the mission and vision as a tool for benchmarking success.

Successful schools consider the challenge of achieving their goals not at the expense of the school culture but as a result of it. So consider this question: Which would you rather have as an administrator: a culture in which all people feel valued and connected, motivated, and cooperative, with reasonably high expectations and incentives, with guidelines to provide consistency and tolerance for uncertainty, or a school in which there are high test scores? Fortunately, the choice does not have to be made, as some might believe it does. There is a way to have both and on top of it all, to have a school with considerably less violence. All this can be a reasonable expectation when the health of the school is the measurement used for the success of the institution.

The term organizational health was first used about 30 years ago to describe the ability of an organization to function effectively, to cope adequately, to change appropriately, and to grow from within. Organizational health can be quantified much like physical health. There are "norms" for what is considered healthy, but it is impossible to define "perfect health" as an absolute. Because of this, we examine each individual and identify what healthy is person by person based on certain continuums, inside of which are expected norms. We often start by looking for symptoms, as the absence of symptoms, for the most part, connotes good physical health. Psychological health, however, may be more complex, as the absence of symptoms is not the only indicator of psychological well-being. An individual who is asymptomatic may still lack fulfillment in his or her life or not be functioning at an optimal level.

Similarly, when we look at the health of an organization, we know problems will always exist in some form, and so a "perfect health" scenario is impossible. As we create the spectrum of norms—no reported violence, for example, or a certain percentage on standardized tests—we still can pay attention to the limitations of our definition.

As a principal in a school with no violence and high test scores, can you be satisfied if there is constant turnover of faculty, poor morale, and an inability to adapt to the changing demands of your district? The principal who has learned to lower his or her expectations may say yes, but the leader who maintains a certain idealism would decline. Thus, an aspiration for eliminating symptoms is too ambiguous to define organizational health. Instead, it may be more important to consider the degree to which these problems will be acceptable, the level of awareness regarding these problems, and the amount of unity in approaching/resolving these issues.

A school system, for instance, may be experiencing symptoms of financial pressure, teacher turnover concerns, and a supply shortage, but if the staff understand and adapt well to these internal and external pressures, working together cooperatively to overcome these issues, a greater degree of organizational health can be achieved. A more fundamental definition of school health is needed to address the complexities of systemic operations.

Organizational health, as it pertains to a school system, can be viewed as the collective awareness of the factors that influence both the internal and external environments, and use of that awareness toward an active pursuit of improvement in areas identified and agreed upon by the collective membership of the constituents within that system. Such improvement would likely lead to the improved efficacy and integrity of that system, by increasing congruence between mission and action, while also expanding on the choices for action within that organization. Furthermore, organizational health is influenced by the way in which subsystems make contact and how the overall system responds to the quality of that contact (Nevis, 1987).

Contact refers to the overlap of boundaries between subsystems and ultimately creates the potential for meaningful exchange across those boundaries. This definition of organizational health is still broad and is difficult to measure. It does, however, leave room for interpretation according to the uniqueness of each organization or setting. Since no two schools are identical, each will develop and measure organizational health through somewhat different processes.

While organizational health within the school system continues to be explored, we find an overlapping of concepts that seem confusing. Terms such as school culture, climate, atmosphere, and environment are often used interchangeably. None of these terms have been inextricably linked to organizational health. This type of comparison may be analogous to comparing, in human anatomy, breathing to the entire respiratory system. One is part of another and not a separate entity, so too is climate a part of an organization's overall health.

As it is important to have a common language when examining organizational health, let's take the following definitions into account as we continue the discussion:

School culture is a combination of the tangible physical, emotional/relational, and environmental dimensions of the institution.

Climate refers to the milieu created by the relationships of faculty, students, and administrators.

Atmosphere is a temporal condition that varies among different groups or subdivisions of the school building and that reflects the tone or tension in that specific location.

Environment has to do with the more tangible conditions of the school, such as cleanliness, safety, and building layout.

All of these concepts will be explored in more depth as part of the three dimensions of organizational health.

An individual's overall health or well-being can be said to be comprised of one's physical, emotional, cognitive, and spiritual states. An organization's overall health is also comprised of the cognitive, emotional, and physical well-being—of the individuals and the organization as a whole.

The cognitive aspect of the organization is represented by the school's ability to adapt to changes in the internal and external environments. The way an organization learns is also part of this cognitive area.

The emotional/relational component is represented by the organization's climate, which is the overall feeling or mood within the institution and the connectedness of the people within.

The physical body is represented through the infrastructure or tangible aspects of the organization, such as the building and its internal and external surroundings.

We will further explore these three dimensions of organizational health: adaptation, climate, and infrastructure. Within the three dimensions, five key attributes will be summarized at the conclusion of each chapter.

CHAPTER 5

Adaptation

Adaptation is the experience and the ability of an organization to meet the changing demands of its internal and external environments. The majority of writing on adaptation has given this term considerable importance in relation to organizational health because adaptation is critically important for the survival of systems. Circumstances may force a system to adapt to a situation that has already arisen (reactive adaptation), while other systems may recognize an opportunity for growth if change occurs (anticipatory adaptation). Whether or not an organization adapts in anticipatory or reactive fashion, the speed and agility with which it responds to the demand for change is important. As the need to adapt arises, and the organization does not respond appropriately, it will become less healthy. Conversely, systems that react too quickly to external and internal pressure with impulsive or even well-intended changes can have adverse consequences as well.

A business cannot be adaptive if its employees are not aware or prepared to adjust. Individuals are more likely to be adaptive if they are encouraged to be creative and appreciated for working hard. In the business world, those companies able to adapt to the changing demands of the marketplace are rewarded by longevity and profit. Schools that learn how to adapt advance themselves to the cutting edge of contemporary education.

Adaptation has been defined as the ability to deal with change. Change, however, is multidimensional, requiring us to better appreciate its diverse nature. There are three major types of organizational change to be familiar with:

Incremental change is derived from a "seize the day" attitude. Change initiatives are intermittent, based upon the need and want at that particular time. With incremental change there tends to be various pictures of success.

Transitional change is focused on realignment and returning to equilibrium.

Transformational change pays greater attention to the path of the organization as opposed to the destination. The nature of change in large part determines how the organization will adapt to the internal and external demands placed upon it.

While the nature of change is variable, we know that the forces for change are being exerted on an organization at all times, so it's not a matter of if change is occurring but what type of change is occurring and how it is being responded to.

Transformational change is the only type of the three that places organizational health at a higher premium. Since schools deal with a product (learning) that cannot be measured by efficiency alone, as is the case with many for profit businesses, it is equally important to consider the pathways that lead to the quality and not just the quantity of learning. When an organization attends to how it is adapting to internal and external pressures, it can become more aware of the possible consequences of whatever actions it is taking. This is an important concept, albeit simple, because of the continuous nature of change and the hidden as well as overt manifestations of conflicts inherent in change.

Let us consider an example to concretize this idea. An elementary school in North Chicago is the temporary station for hundreds of military families. They sometimes withdraw their children from school just months after enrolling them, due to deployment or other relocations. Due to this continuous movement the school developed a policy that students will be placed in the most basic classes until their records arrive (this sometimes takes weeks). The consequence of this action is oftentimes frustration on the part of the student who is already finding acclimation challenging. Teachers are prepared for the possible outcome of this action and are prepared to adapt the material given to the student.

This is a relatively simple but helpful example of transitional change and how being aware can help the adaptation process. Without this awareness a school can be caught off guard by unexpected changes, leading faculty to exist in a perpetual state of crisis or catching up.

If we buy into the notion that organizations, like people, are always in a state of becoming, we can appreciate that movement is occurring along various continua. At the end of each continuum is the polarity that defines it, such as cohesion and fragmentation or structured versus unstructured. Adaptation can be examined as the movement along this continuum and how this movement is a response to the demands placed upon an organization. Three key concepts are described below that come under the heading of adaptation, including the one just discussed—awareness.

Awareness, or an appreciation for scanning one's environment, is an important component in how an organization adapts. If organizational leaders appreciate where they exist along various continua, they can better plan for where changes may be needed. Movement toward a particular polarity is determined in large part by the organization's attitude toward ambivalence, or in other words, its *resistance*.

Learning is both the product of adaptation and an influential determinant for how the organization adapts to change, and subsequently on the direction toward polarities. How well does the school appreciate the change that is taking place and what information is pulled from this experience?

Resiliency is the measure of how well an organization tolerates movement away from its desired goals either by design or by happenstance.

AWARENESS AS A FUNCTION OF ADAPTATION

When we explore the nature of awareness, what we are actually looking at is the degree to which the organizational leaders are appreciative of resistance. Resistance is a naturally occurring by-product of personal interaction that affects an organization's ability to adapt beyond simple survival. To understand resistance we can appreciate the dichotomy of forces that act upon an organization when change is taking place. One force propels change, while the other force propels persistence or sameness.

Resistance can be found at all times in varying degrees, within every organization, and at times, may be an indicator that change is not appropriate. At other times resistance is about the fear of change, even when the change would possibly be beneficial or at least inevitable. If we look at resistance as a natural process that requires a fuller understanding of what is, we can normalize conflict within or between organizational structures. Understanding each of the opposing force fields is important to improving organizational awareness and ultimately the ability to adapt to change.

Here is an example of resistance at work in a school that has limited awareness of its existence: A small elementary school in southern New Jersey has a no-tolerance policy on bullying. A young girl is suspended for pushing a fellow student. What the administrator is not aware of is how this act was a response to being picked on for several weeks prior to the incident leading to the suspension. The parents of this young girl go to the school to complain about this "unjust" policy and ask the principal to reconsider. Upon hearing the full story, the principal changes her decision, which then brings the other child's parents in to complain. "How can you just change a policy when you feel like it . . . what about what happened to our daughter?"

Frustrated by the perceived injustice, the parents go the school superintendent who reinforces the principal's decision in public but questions it in private. The teachers in the school become split about this apparent bending of the rules and tension grows. While the tension may or may not create problems within the school, it is going to move the school further along the continuum toward fragmentation.

For those educators reading this scenario you may wonder what could have been done differently to prevent the same outcome. First, for anybody who has been in the position of making decisions that affect others, you know that residual fallout is common. Not everybody will be pleased with the outcome of your action, and those who experience displeasure may harbor ill feelings.

Acknowledging the differences of opinion, even when you don't believe others have a right to voice their dissent, is helpful to lessen the intensity of their displeasure. During a staff meeting for instance, the principal can bring the issue up and ask for feedback, giving the impression he or she is receptive to other viewpoints that could impact future decision making. Many leaders refrain from opening up this "can of worms" because they are fearful it will invite criticism or give permission to others to challenge their authority. In fact it does quite the opposite. A school culture where students and faculty can feel heard in public helps lessen their need to be subversive in private.

Resistance is often labeled as the problem, when in fact the reaction to the resistance may actually be problematic. Resistance can lead to stifled organizational growth when communication and problem solving become interrupted. Since resistance is avoidance of contact across the boundaries between subsystems, polarization can occur. Subgroups move toward opposite extremes and erect rigid boundaries, which can lead to power struggles as if each side were the adversary.

Boundaries allow groups and individuals the opportunity for exchange unless they are rigid and impermeable. For the individual, contact across the boundaries can be the internal process of experiencing the self or others. Within an organization it can be the management of a boundary between self and others, or between subsystems, that influences the quantity and quality of the resistance. In other words, while resistance promotes persistence, it also mobilizes energy in the face of a perceived or real threat. As a result, while the individual or organization resists change, unknowingly, true exploration of oneself or one's environment will be avoided. The way in which this contact is avoided helps to define the contact style of the individual or organization.

Just as an individual uses defense mechanisms to avoid experiencing painful stimuli, so too do organizations develop styles that may limit contact. The organizational style is heavily influenced by the style of the leadership. Projection is a prime example of a commonly used contact style that allows the individual or organization to interpret resistance as opposition rather than a natural force to preserve sameness. Administrators are labeled as uncaring, while unions are viewed as oppositional. Both groups define the other in terms of their own negative perception of the other's resistance.

This style filters down to students, as can be exemplified by a student who is labeled as disruptive when not getting his or her needs met. In this case, the school will often use punishment to exercise its control, believing this is the best method for gaining cooperation. Since unions and administration are more equally weighted in power, no such punitive measures can resolve problems, and agreement or at least cooperation will have to be found by other methods.

Within organizations, there is rarely absolute agreement toward any change; instead there is generally resistance to an aspect of that change in each person or group. To circumvent this, include those people who are potentially resisters at the start of an initiative, as well as in the discussion of from whom resistance might come and why. In order for this to be an effective strategy, those initiating the change will need to see resistance as a process that, if embraced and treated accordingly, can produce solid results with greater buy-in.

In large organizations, there are more levels and subsystems, meaning more complexity in the change process. Since resistance can be divisive within a school, larger school systems have a greater challenge to remain integrated. Being integrated means that each of the subsystems working more harmoniously (less stagnation from resistance) rather than as adversaries (greater stagnation from resistance).

With multiple systems, each having unique objectives and potentially different agendas, the potential for competition over resources can influence how the system as a whole remains fully integrated.

A large school system with multiple elementary, middle, and high schools, for instance, has a greater number of subsystems, each with its own focus and agenda. When the state of New Jersey moved to a standardized curriculum, the larger school systems would likely have had greater difficulty adapting to this change because of the greater diversity of existing curricula within the district and thus more opportunity for resistance to thwart the change effort. A smaller school system may be able to enact these changes with greater ease, as awareness requires less energy and overall work.

However, large school systems do have some advantages when it comes to adaptation because of the greater resources within that system. If, for instance, the school were mandated to initiate a standardized curriculum without increasing the budget for new textbooks, the larger system would have a larger number of staff members with potentially more resources from which to draw.

As stated above, different and possibly opposing forces often impact adaptation. A school district is under constant pressure to meet the changing demands of both its internal and external environments. The pressure to address internal issues is typically generated from unions, employee wants, management goals, or leadership from within the district. External pressures are those concerns that may be evoked or raised by community changes, parental attitudes, legislative changes, media pressure, and other community events. Recent changes in curriculum throughout the state of New Jersey, as discussed earlier, are an example of an external pressure to which each school can adapt.

As with adaptation, schools can look at the impact of resistance to change that occurs as a result of a reactive or anticipatory situation. Anticipatory change often allows for more planning and gaining insight from resistors. Reactive change leads to concern about the reason for change and can often be the catalyst for resistance. Additionally, there are inventive changes (changes initiated to support effectiveness of the entire system), which tend to be less divisive than changes motivated by a personal position. In this case, the focus of the organization shifts to the whole rather than any one part.

Resistance is best understood as a construct within the *paradoxical theory of change*. This theory suggests that organizations must fully embrace what is before recognizing or pursuing what may be. For example, a school that is plagued by bullying would be encouraged to fully understand the etiology of the problem, rather than taking a reactionary stance of finding immediate solutions.

Understanding the perspectives of the school, faculty, and administrators regarding causative factors for problems such as violence, high teacher turnover, and a lack of qualified applicants coming into the system are important issues in understanding organizational health. The idea behind increasing awareness is that an organization will then better understand polarities and where they exist on each of those continua. Once they have a greater awareness of where they currently rest on any such continuum, they can decide collectively, if this is where they want to be in order to deal with the problem with which they are contending.

With regard to teacher turnover, for example, if a particular school is high in structure but low in autonomy, they will be more thoughtful about the new teachers they interview for open positions. They may also prepare incoming teachers to better understand the culture in which they are deciding to participate.

The paradoxical theory of change also suggests that in examining polarities we begin to understand where we are located on the continuum and how we may position ourselves. If we recognize polarities as important for maintaining balance, we can view resistance as a creative force that attempts to maintain equilibrium. For change to occur, however, this equilibrium will be disrupted, at least temporarily.

Only those organizations that attend to how this disruption is experienced by the different subsystems will likely experience successful change. Change is difficult for those within the organization because it disrupts a familiar pattern of expectation. When this occurs, both anxiety and excitement may be increased. Those organizations that are aware of and open to the perceived changes, can foster excitement and reduce anxiety.

RESILIENCY AS A FUNCTION OF ADAPTATION

The ability to adapt to these combined internal and external pressures is determined in part by the resiliency of the institution. Resiliency has to do with the school's awareness about their style of adaptation but also their willingness and ability to adjust this style as needed. Schools that are highly resilient are likely to have a solid infrastructure and supportive climate. With a solid infrastructure and supportive climate, schools may be less reactive and more anticipatory about their change efforts. When they do need to respond unexpectedly to a change initiative, a resilient school will perceive less disruption and therefore be better equipped to resume fluid operations.

Resiliency may either be a willingness to remain steadfast when there is pressure to conform or it can be the courage to make changes even when it is unpopular. Resiliency can be any of the following:

- Flexible to accommodate differing opinions;
- Tolerant of diversity;
- Inclusive rather than exclusive;
- Encouraging of open and direct contact;
- Acknowledging shortcomings or limitations.

Not enough is known about what makes some schools more resilient than others, why some schools have low turnover and high morale, or why violence is a seldom used alternative to solving problems. If we go under the assumption that resiliency extends beyond the resources of finances, we will appreciate how many other variants can influence a highly adaptive school. In fact, it is often those schools that have less money that bond together to become highly adaptive.

Consider the following example in appreciating the resiliency of a given school. NDHS is a fairly large high school with over 2,000 students. The principal is relatively new, having taken over only a year prior. She was brought in because the school was considered to be going "down hill," and the pressure on the superintendent was growing. The original plan for the school was to handle the overload for the other overcrowded schools in the district.

Among other problems at the time the principal took over were high faculty turnover, poor morale, and a significant increase in student violence. In fact the threat of violence had grown so high that teachers were afraid to come to work and substitutes were hard to find. There were occasions where classes were uncovered altogether.

Outrage from the parents attracted media attention, and news reports quickly began berating the district with articles about incompetence. For a school that was touted as "cutting edge" when it was first designed, not more than 15 years prior, was now being condemned as an atrocity. Those few parents who could afford private schools pulled their children out while others used alternative addresses to enroll in neighboring schools. It was quickly becoming a quagmire for controversy.

The administration at the time was trying desperately to stay afloat. They described their situation as an endless choice of lesser evils. Do we tighten restrictions on faculty, forcing them into greater accountability, which surely ran the risk of losing more staff? Do we heighten security spending the funds that could be geared toward more creative programming? Do we remove graffiti from the walls to make the environment more hospitable, knowing it will be up again in a matter of days? In the end, little was done to energize the school. Traditional beliefs held by veteran faculty prevented much in the way of innovation.

Stagnation helped the school and all of its members feel as though they were stuck in the mud. Like a car that's spinning its wheels and spewing out dirt from behind, covering everything with muck, if an organization remains stuck for too long, as this school did, organizational breakdown begins. Fingers get pointed as people look for scapegoats while insulating themselves from responsibility. Administration blames teachers, teachers blame administration, and the parents blame the school. Communication becomes less direct as cliques begin to form. An atmosphere of suspicion causes faculty to isolate themselves. Like a cup of water filled to the very top, it only takes a drop to make it spill over.

Resiliency is compromised because the school exists on the breaking point, not an uncommon experience for schools struggling with limited funding and extreme external pressure. In fact, had it not been for the media pressure and a superintendent mindful of his own political standing, nothing would have changed.

But change did happen and it came in dramatic fashion. The principal was replaced and that was just the beginning. Policies and procedures were altered and created but done so unilaterally. New staff were brought in that were loyal to the principal while tenured teachers became more ambivalent, anticipating retirement. Money was given to the school by the district to help ensure the principal would be successful in her quest to revive the dying institution; however, this created more power struggles because of allocation.

Unfortunately, change came too quickly. The climate of the school went from insecure to paranoid, while chaos turned to rigidity. What was a fairly autonomous environment was now more dictative. Ironically, the attempts to build greater resiliency wound up ineffective. It demonstrated that neither end of any continuum is conducive to improving tolerance to deal with the internal or external pressure a school experiences.

Fortunately for NDHS, the principal was able to scan the environment, recognizing the limitations of her approach. She became increasingly receptive to the input from veteran teachers, slowly gaining their trust. She appreciated their resistance as a need to hold on to something of importance as opposed to a threat to her leadership. Decision making became more of a shared process and even though changes occurred more slowly, there was greater buy-in to the changes on an organizational level. The resiliency of the school began to improve.

LEARNING AS A FUNCTION OF ADAPTATION

The style in which an organization learns has an impact on its capacity to adapt. A school system is no exception, particularly because learning is the primary objective of every district. Schools throughout history have adapted their teaching approach according to different learning theories, such as whole language, multiple stimulus fields, and experiential methods. It's common practice to utilize the most contemporary research on teaching methods. In fact, a high percentage of teacher in-services are geared toward the latest and greatest teaching fad.

Student learning is important for academic success, while institutional learning is important for organizational health. How the institution itself learns (the constituents within) often goes unrecognized by those responsible for providing the instruction. Learning is a component of adaptation in that the results of intended or unintended change produce effects, which may or may not be attended to by the organization. The information, and subsequently conclusions, formed by the organization following evaluation of the changes and impact thereof reflects the learning of that organization. Organizations that perceive learning as a high priority will likely be more able to anticipate obstacles for future success and therefore be more highly adaptable.

This may be more difficult for schools compared to consumer and product-based industries, since there is less immediate feedback to measure how adaptation is taking place. If, for instance, the soda companies learn that American trends are moving toward a healthier lifestyle through improved nutrition, they may see a decline in sales, which their research and development department will analyze. The information is then given to the marketing department, which can change the nature of advertising or even product development. Traditional businesses can use a variety of measures to indicate success. Generally speaking, the success of the industry is measured in net profit; however, there are other indicators such as client satisfaction, product innovation, waste elimination to improve efficiency, and financial growth. In corporations, feedback loops are generated to constantly monitor organizational functioning. This is not the case with nonprofit organizations such as schools, which operate under more restrictive financial limitations. Schools believe they cannot measure success through the more sophisticated measures used by corporations and others smaller businesses.

How then do schools measure their success? According to the legislative bodies schools are forced to rely on measures such as standardized testing as a solitary means of assessment. However, such measures provide little understanding of the educational system nor do they result in changes addressing integral concerns and problems such as student violence. Measurement must also include the intangibles of social learning such as moral reasoning, conflict negotiation, and general social skill development. Adding to the degree of difficulty, this measurement will change according to the level of internal and external pressure a school faces on a daily basis. Schools that are well supported by their district and community are freer to consider this question.

Since the majority of schools in this country face extraordinary pressure to succeed according to norms they themselves have not established, organizational improvement has given way to stagnation. It seems that schools do not seek transformational change, but rather seek transitional or incremental change, as directed by those in positions of power, creating fewer opportunities for learning.

The success of an agency depends in large part upon the organization's willingness and ability to be self-aware and then use that awareness for positive growth. A basic assumption of the Gestalt Institute of Cleveland, a pioneer in the instruction of organizational consultants is:

> The reason one group or organization excels over another given equitable resources is the ability or competency of being able to scan one's internal and external environment, make meaning of the data

> collected and respond appropriately in ways that support reaching
> agreed upon desired outcomes. (Nevis, 1987, p. 14)

Additionally, organizational health depends largely on each individual's ability to regulate him- or herself in response to his or her working environment.

There is some level of awareness of what schools are experiencing because some changes are taking place. A number of structural changes, in an attempt to make schools safer, such as metal detectors, have been installed in some urban city schools, bullying prevention and peer mediation programs have been created, and crisis response teams were established to deal with violence after the fact. The above-mentioned changes may be beneficial, although they are only a part of the remedy.

The psychological definition of learning is the modification of behavior based on experience. In seeing the types of changes that have occurred in school systems throughout the country, we perhaps have a better understanding of how schools understand school violence and how they respond to lessons of experience by making less than comprehensive changes. Based on the above definition, installation of metal detectors and peer mediation programs show schools are learning. The demand for schools to modify their behavior in the most appropriate way, however, is crucial to adapting to current challenges such as student violence.

The quality and quantity of learning that takes place within any organization is modulated by the willingness or receptiveness to new information. Whether the information is being derived internally or externally, there should be a process by which new ideas are developed and accepted as important to organizational growth.

Learning may be a primary mechanism for how organizations adapt to their internal and external environments. While some aspects of the change process are less conscious, such as that which is more reactionary or impulsive, learning represents change that is intentional. Given this notion, it seems important to further explore how this process works.

While schools may be institutions for learning, they are not often institutions that are aware of how *they* learn. Schools, like other organizations, are inanimate organisms wherein change may occur, but schools themselves are often not viewed as being able to change or grow. Change, within such institutions, may be directed or undirected, purposeful or accidental, and utilized or ignored.

Regardless of the environment the school is located within, there is added pressure for success because of the consistent demand for success from parents, state boards, district officials, and legislators. A lack of resources is not a sufficient reason in the eyes of some for poor performance. Energy that is put into improving the quality of standards may not be invested in understanding the reasons for student performance. Student achievement may not be a comprehensive measure of school functioning because it does not take into account the intangible learning that takes place in schools. Without recognition of what standards fail to capture, it will remain the measuring stick by which schools are held accountable.

In order for organizations to improve their fluidity of learning, a climate of openness is important to facilitate the free exchange of ideas. Without reciprocal feedback loops that exist in organizations where growth and development are promoted, stagnation will likely occur because no formal mechanism for learning exists.

The learning process may be misunderstood or not understood well enough by school administrators, as it pertains to the organization itself. First, administrators may perceive schools as not possessing the capacity for learning, and second, they may believe the focus of the school faculty is teaching, while learning is reserved for the students.

Such is the case with other social service agencies whose products are people-oriented services. In these public or private, profit or nonprofit organizations, the emphasis is on service delivery to the target population with less consideration for the staff delivering the services. If school administrators had a greater awareness of the importance of teacher efficacy with regard to student learning, they may be in a better position to make choices regarding the operations of the school.

Consider the teacher who spends his or her own money to provide needed supplies for the students and does not get reimbursed due to budget constraints. If this principal were to implement a policy of teacher recognition, efficacy may offset the resentment experienced by the paucity of adequate supplies. Without awareness for the impact of rewards and incentives for teachers, burnout and turnover become more significant.

What does all this have to do with student violence, you might now ask? The simple answer is that we are not learning from our experience. Even with the catastrophic violent events of the past 10 years, we seem to have learned that metal detectors and bullying prevention programs are the answers. Our response as a nation to this epidemic indicates that we have successfully analyzed the data from the past decade. This is not the entire fault of the school because it reflects the way our educational system learns. We too often make hasty decisions based on end results without a full appreciation for what is. Due to the pressure once again from media, the politicians, and families, we are rushed into quick fixes that do not address the full scope of the problem.

FIVE CRITICAL ASPECTS OF ADAPTATION

Professional growth and development is the most underutilized tool in the schools' arsenal to improve their ability to adapt. This required activity that offers the opportunity for learning is often looked upon as a meaningless exercise that either wastes the teachers time or serves to create more work. Those workplaces that support their employees by providing opportunities for stimulation and learning will likely find an environment with a greater aptitude for creativity and improved productivity. Unfortunately, in many school districts training is looked upon with apathy. This may in part be due to the lack of quality training, the lack of input into the training, and the fact that cost cutting in schools usually targets this area first.

There is a certain irony that schools, institutions for learning, don't often value their professional growth and development. In schools where this is the case, stagnation may occur, which is a precursor to organizational breakdown. Whether it's due to a political agenda, a lack of preparation (due to time/monetary constraints), or an overzealous leader attempting to promote change, staff training is not being utilized to its fullest capacity.

Schools that are highly resilient and able to adapt to internal/external pressure find a way of using staff training time as a vehicle for increasing awareness. Teachers, even more than most, dislike being told what to do. They are the experts of their children and often take great pride in student education. Training that stimulates thinking and expands perception far outweighs presentations that introduce the newest strategy or technique for teaching. Training that involves the teachers in some way from the onset, whether through their own research or experience, gains more appreciation and interest.

Staff development that balances content with process will also find greater success. Similar to staff meetings that allow for reciprocal feedback, training needs to be interactive. Teachers learn much the same way students do in terms of needing an experiential component to concretize the lesson.

Decision making is the process by which conflicts are resolved, plans are made, and goals are formed. This is the time where faculty will negotiate their wants and needs, balancing them against each other as well as the school. Decision making is both a formal and informal process, depending upon the nature of the choice being made. Formal decision making involves meetings in which all the relevant parties are present and there is an exchange of ideas. Informal decision making tends to be more unilateral and doesn't involve as much attention to procedure. Both methods are most successful when communication is open and direct.

The way in which administration and faculty reach conclusions around problems, conflicts, and other important issues will affect the overall milieu of the workplace. Top-down decision making for instance, may lead to front-line employees feeling less valued and thus investing less energy in problem solving. The strategies for existing prevention programs represent this style of decision making. Teachers are not typically consulted about what types of prevention strategies are chosen or how they are implemented. We know that without the involvement of people at each level, in the earlier stages of decision making, any strategy is less likely to be owned and accepted by those out of the loop.

Whether those excluded from the process sabotage the plan or simply don't invest much energy in its success, the fabric of the system begins to erode. It becomes one more job-related frustration or disappointment that pushes an individual to become more indifferent. Ambivalence or indifference toward the workplace helps schools become less tolerant of change and therefore less adaptive.

Conversely, in schools where teachers feel a part of the decision-making process, there is greater energy to deal with strife. More people invested means greater creativity in problem solving.

Teamwork will play a role in adaptation because it relates directly to competition, trust, and support. In a workplace where constructive teamwork is consistent, employees will likely be more relaxed and encouraged. In a workplace filled with a "cutthroat" atmosphere, employees may be more guarded and isolated.

Here is an example of how effective teamwork helps a school to be more adaptive. A middle school in southern New Jersey has teams called "families" that comprise a counselor, teachers, and a support person, all for the same grade level. This group is responsible for every aspect of the child's educational programming, including social growth. If a child begins to show signs of problems, such as grade decline, mood shift, or absenteeism, the team quickly goes into motion. They compare observations and begin planning in advance of a more significant problem.

Teamwork helps faculty feel more powerful and effectual. In numbers there is a stronger voice than standing alone. There is also more satisfaction in teaming issues because of the energy that is generated from the group process. The obstacles to this approach include greater complexity and subgrouping, both of which can diminish the school's adaptability.

Greater complexity means that differing viewpoints stretch the team in different directions. Conflicts are more likely to occur when disagreements do not get resolved. An appreciation for group dynamics can be helpful in negotiating this inevitability. Recognizing roles and having procedures in place to manage differences will help. In addition to helping with adaptation, strong teamwork will also have a strong influence on the climate of the school.

Supervision affects the degree of adaptation through the quality and quantity of oversight, direction, and support the leadership provides. Workplaces with little feedback and direction may yield environments that are chaotic, confusing, and lacking in a sense of appreciation. Conversely, in workplaces where supervision is readily available and useful to the employees, accountability and clarity may be increased.

Supervision is one of the first casualties of a busy administrator. For an average school with more than 30 teachers, consider how much time it would take to have regular supervisory meetings. It's simply not practical to afford that kind of time, so what usually happens are informal conversations, mixed with occasional formal observations.

Supervision is made increasingly difficult when teachers and other faculty are less receptive to feedback. If a school leader is less skilled in providing constructive feedback or a teacher feels threatened, then the result is polarization. These situations can quickly escalate into adversarial relationships in which extreme antipathy is not unheard of. The deeper the animosity the further people move away from the concerns of the team and the desired goal of collaboration.

The *structure* of a workplace has a more observable impact on their capacity to adapt. Loosely structured systems, in which faculty and students have tremendous freedom to act independently, will adapt differently than a tightly controlled, highly organized system. In an effort to help differentiate the role of structure we will contrast the two ends of the continuum.

School A has few policies and procedures, and the ones it does have are not consistently enforced. Teachers have permission to run their classrooms as they see fit, and staff meetings are more like informal parties. The faculty generally enjoys one another and may even socialize outside of school. Autonomy and creativity are high, although there is little consistency from day to day. When the need for change comes about, generally from external pressure, disorganization and confusion occur, making the entire process fairly inefficient.

School B has policies and procedures for nearly any potential issue, and they are enforced rigidly. There is little room for individual differences since much of the day is standardized. Each class within a grade does the same lessons, which overlap with other subjects. Due to the high organization and consistency, faculty and students alike find their days predictable—and dull. The need for change may stem from a desire for individuation, not something that is encouraged or dealt with easily by the school. Such wants are perceived as threats to the integrity of the institution and are met with strong opposition.

While both of these examples are exaggerations of opposite polarities, they demonstrate how organizational structure can help or hinder adaptation. Each school exists somewhere along this and other continua, experiencing self-imposed obstacles to flexing with change.

CHAPTER 6

Climate

Organizational climate is a frequently used term in the organizational development and school reform literature, but it lacks a clear definition. Climate is a specific component of an organizational culture that deals with the mood or milieu of the organization, although consensus on meaning has not yet been found. Differentiation between culture and climate is important to help the numerous educators, practitioners, and researchers who continue to use these concepts interchangeably.

It was previously mentioned that atmosphere is similar to climate, although it is shorter lived and less pervasive. If we compare a school organization to an individual, we may substitute atmosphere for mood and climate for temperament. Thus, climate can be considered the collection and interaction of the various moods of individuals within the school. Because individuals make up subsystems (such as the English department), we must also pay attention to how the various moods of the subsystems are interacting with each other. The method by which various systems interrelate to satisfy both the needs of the organization and the individual also accounts for the climate of the organization.

Climate has been referred to as the personality of the school. While research suggests that the climate of a school may be either open or closed, the idea of the continuum rather than an absolute allows for greater potential. In a school with a more open climate, we find more dedicated faculty, supportive leadership, and strong communication.

A closed system promotes greater polarization and disharmony. A school is neither open nor closed but somewhere along a continuum, which leaves room for movement toward a particular polarity, depending upon the conditions influencing the school and the way in which the school adapts to these pressures. The pressures may be external, such as political pressures from the state board of education, or they may be internal. Internal pressure would include the influences of interactions between various subsystems within the organization.

The interrelated systems within an organization include the individual, the group(s), and the whole. There are many individuals and many groups, but only one whole, and the whole is always greater than the sum of its parts. This means the collective experience and interaction of each of the subsystems creates an overall whole. This whole cannot be broken into equal parts because together it is more. The secretarial staff may be disenchanted with their jobs, while the teachers are very content on the whole. How could we anticipate the overall mood of the school? We could describe each subgroup separately, but even this would not be quite accurate, since the two subgroups influence the whole by their interactions.

Another example is found when examining the various departments within an urban school in New York City. The social studies department has its experience of the school, which for this example we will assume is very positive. They always recruit the most experienced teachers in the field and have an operating budget that meets the department's needs. They are all well liked by the principal and in good standing with the students. By contrast, the English department is severely understaffed, has the poorest test scores of all the community schools, and feels great pressure from the principal. While both of these experiences are known throughout the school, the whole system has a combined experience of these two parts. The competition that exists between these two departments creates a tension within the school that is felt by those within and outside these two departments and by the students themselves.

If in either of these two examples there was encouragement to attend on a systems level to the relationships between these departments, interventions could have been devised to improve the climate. Not having an awareness of these conflicts or not attending to them is one way to breed contempt that eventually filters down to the students. Just as organizational health reflects a willingness to scan the internal and external environments, climate is the outcome of this awareness. Schools with limited awareness of their internal and external environments may exhibit a higher tolerance for disparaging interpersonal encounters, not because they condone this behavior, but rather because they are uncertain as to the etiology. A school, for instance, that is high on structure may find staff members who feel a lack of autonomy. Awareness of how climate is created helps improve the ability to influence it.

In the case of school systems, despite whether the ability or competency to scan one's internal or external environment exists, the data collected must be acted upon in order to reach a goal. It is not enough to recognize and acknowledge this premise in theory; action must be taken for desired results to be seen. In the case of job satisfaction surveys, for instance, giving them to faculty and not using the results actually does more harm, because employees are reminded of the perceived indifference of their administration.

CYCLE OF EXPERIENCE

There have been several references to scanning the internal and external environments, coming from a basic underlying premise that each individual, group, and organization functions along a cycle of experience. For an individual, this cycle begins with a sensation, while for the organization it begins with the scanning process. From sensation comes awareness, the key ingredient in both individual and organizational health. Awareness is the act of attending to one's individual sensations and experiences, or in the case of an organization, awareness refers to the process of conceptualizing the data found during the scanning process. Without awareness, individuals will respond to stimuli in a less than conscious reaction, while organizations will lose valuable information that can guide the actions, direction, and mission.

From awareness comes rising energy leading to an action. In the case of organizations, there must be a commitment to the energy before any movement or action can take place. In the case of organizations, this action may be an attempt to mobilize energy and interest in ideas or proposals or any attempt to identify differences and conflicts or competing interests.

For instance, consider a teacher who, after paying attention to the pervasive boredom of faculty during staff meetings, suggests that the staff select the training topics, instead of the principal. Before there is movement toward this suggestion, energy will be created and committed to by the group. If there is disagreement among the faculty regarding this idea, this conflict must be dealt with openly before any successful resolution can take place. Certainly the principal can intrude his or her decision upon the group, but this will not help alleviate the boredom; in fact it may strengthen the resistance of faculty who did not feel heard.

Organizational energy can look similar to an electroencephalogram, which measures heart rhythm. There are spikes, which represent the rising energy from an idea or conflict, occurring frequently but not often systematically. Some of these spikes in energy may lead to an action, but many fade as quickly as they are formed.

With energy formation and action come some form of contact. For organizations this may be joining together in working toward a common objective or understanding the nature of a problem. While there isn't always agreement for a course of action, there will be a change in boundaries as a result of this movement. At this point in time, boundaries extend from individuals in subgroups to others in the same or other subgroups. The result of boundary contact may be friction, confluence, or ambivalence, all of which create experiences for all involved. For contact to be made, however, there still must be a commitment of energy from the organizational unit or subsystem. In hierarchal systems, the leader or supervisor will ultimately give his or her approval. In more autocratic groups, consensus is typically the method of committing energy.

Following contact is resolution or closure on the individual level and assessment on the organizational level. In this part of the cycle of experience, there may be acknowledgment of what has occurred and what still needs to be done. All too often, organizations do not reflect upon the action and boundary shift that have taken place, leaving them susceptible to move toward a pole that is less desired. For instance, a faculty that decides to implement a rotational system for staff development, in order to increase stimulation, may not realize that the resentment of added responsibilities could begin to sabotage the training process further. If schools would pay closer attention to assessing their action plans, greater learning will take place about their decision making.

The cycle of experience is important on an individual level as well, in that it helps us understand whether a person or group is making contact both with themselves and with others. How contact is made determines the connectedness of those in the relationship. Intimacy is a direct result of the depth of contact and the fullness of experience between self in relation to other. Contact with oneself is the process by which an individual becomes aware of a sensation within the body and moves to assimilate the information gained from this awareness: for instance, a student who recognizes the reason for not doing homework has to do with rebellion against his or her parents. Contact between groups is the process by which subsystems form a shared picture or desired outcome for pursuing objectives.

If the principal of a particular school is interested in addressing an escalation in behavioral problems within his or her school, the principal's ability to make contact with the subgroup of faculty responsible for this objective is crucial. With only partial contact, ideas may meet with misunderstanding or even outright resentment, because they were not fully embraced by those who needed to carry out the plan. There is no guarantee that contact will help gain agreement on the idea, but it will certainly help with that potential, by decreasing resistance.

Additionally, it is important to attend to the systemic issues, which always play a role in the creation of behavioral problems.

Take into account the developmental stage of adolescence, a time in which young people are attempting to establish their autonomy and independence. Now consider this stage in relation to a typical classroom setting. Such settings, expecting order and discipline, are often overlooked as an inherent conflict within the system. Without attending to the specific issue within the context of the larger picture, such as antagonistic relationships between teachers and students, contact between subgroups (teachers, students, administrators) is lessened and resistance is increased.

Contact or the feeling of connectivity is vital to the creation of an open climate for both students and faculty. Relationships are formed based on a number of variables, including the application and dissemination of power and control. In typical hierarchical organizations, those nearest the top of the pyramid increasingly hold power and control. Those with power in a school system make the decisions or at least control the process by which decisions are made. In school systems, the principal is clearly at the top of the school pyramid, which may be expanded to a larger pyramid including the superintendent, the school board, the regional superintendent, and so forth. Important decisions such as what school district you get employed by is often a result of who you know and how much power that person yields. Those with less power oftentimes become resentful and resistant within the school, thereby altering the climate within that school system.

Hierarchical systems are modeled for the students who also assume like social structures. Bullies thrive off of top-down strata, overpowering those beneath them. Students unfortunate enough to be at the bottom of the pyramid become victimized, occasionally becoming perpetrators themselves. Catastrophic violence as we have been witness to in the past decade is almost always a result of the victim becoming the perpetrator.

FIVE KEY ASPECTS OF CLIMATE

Morale can be a result of climate and it can be a determinant of climate as well. Internal and external events influence the mood of employees individually and collectively. For instance, in schools where violent episodes occur with a higher frequency toward teachers, the morale of the teachers would likely decline. The morale of the employees weighs heavily on the overall climate of the school by influencing attitudes and behavior. Attitudes may become more dismissive toward student issues, since they are not feeling as though their basic need for safety is being met.

Morale is rarely addressed as an important issue in schools, perhaps because it is believed that there is little administration can do to affect the level. With underpaid teachers and a lack of adequate resources, we may set the bar of expectations too low with regard to how faculty feel about their jobs. In addition, being social service workers who are drawn to this field by our compassion and interest in helping children, we take for granted the motivation to stay in the profession.

Morale is different from job satisfaction as it's more of a collective force as opposed to an individualized variable. Morale is the combined sense of appreciation and value that faculty hold for their work. It is the inspiration that creates energy for dealing with the increasing demands of the job. Morale determined in part the extra degree to which faculty will extend themselves beyond what is expected of them for their job.

This is a very difficult factor to control because it lies outside the scope of any one person, whether that is an administrator, secretary, school board member, or superintendent. Morale can ebb and flow but on the whole requires continuous effort to sustain. The challenge in environments that are admittedly student focused is helping the faculty feel like they matter as well. Morale is most heavily affected by factors of adaptation such as decision making, teamwork, and supervision.

Job satisfaction has very direct implications for school climate. Many factors go into job satisfaction, some of which are in the control of administration and some are not. Salaries, geographic location, job benefits are all relatively stable variables that will help determine how an educator feels about his or her job. Other determinants such as relationships with coworkers, administrators, and students will also make a difference.

In a workplace where employees do not feel appreciated or valued, interactions with each other or the students will be adversely affected. In a 1997 survey by the National Center for Education Statistics, teachers identified job satisfaction most closely associated with: administrative support and leadership, good student behavior, a positive school atmosphere, and teacher autonomy. It is clear from this feedback that the factors described here for organizational culture are closely interrelated and therefore must be examined collectively.

Philosophical accord impacts climate because the actions of employees and students are guided in part by ideological principle. If a large enough group of faculty experience disharmony with these ideological principles or the implementation of them, there may be a disturbance experienced throughout the workplace. Philosophical accord is the agreement with the espoused values of the school by faculty of that school, including the administrators, support personnel, and teaching faculty. In a school system, the agreement by the collective faculty with the direction of the school is important for unity. It is this unity that will provide more efficiency, a stronger peer culture, and greater job satisfaction of the faculty.

Without a strong philosophical accord, faculty will have difficulty in obtaining a sense of meaningfulness and purpose about their work. Outright disagreement with values, actions, and philosophy can further destabilize a school environment. A school's zero-tolerance policy is a good example of a contested value within many school systems across the nation. Whereas many teachers may feel safe with the belief that punishment needs to be swift and unbending, others may argue that expediency should not be sacrificed for sensibility. If there is enough disagreement within a school's faculty, the culture of that school would be adversely affected.

It may be said that while the policies/procedures, mission/vision, and espoused values comprise much of the school's ideological infrastructure, the philosophical accord is the measure of these principles, as seen by the attitudes of the employees and students.

Communication among faculty is an important component of climate, in that direct, open, and two-way dialogue will improve every other aspect of school culture including the infrastructure and adaptation. Communication is a tool that can widely influence the relationships within the school. Direct communication that is expressed and received successfully will help people know where they stand with one another. Conversely, indirect communication that is neither expressed nor received openly will help create tension, not allowing for negotiation and compromise. Without effective and efficient communication, organizations may find increased politicking among the staff, which disrupts the working environment.

Communication problems typically occur because people are unable or unwilling to tolerate differences. When people feel challenged or threatened, they resort to withdrawal or they may turn to others with whom they know they will receive agreement. Teacher cafeterias are common meeting grounds for venting and gossiping, two forms of communication that often create more problems than they resolve.

Although administrators cannot control the way in which faculty communicate with one another, they can model more healthy forms of dialogue. By expressing messages with ownership, such as "I am upset by your actions," instead of "you should never have . . .," makes a significant difference because defensiveness is lessened. Receiving messages through reflective listening, such as "I hear that you are upset with me for . . . ," helps people feel heard, and again reduces defensiveness.

Autonomy and *empowerment* are related factors within any work environment. The degree to which an employee is encouraged to work freely with adequate support influences the climate of the workplace. Particularly restrictive environments without autonomy yield a distinctly different cultural effect than those workplaces that encourage creativity and freedom.

Autonomy differs from structure in that one has to do with the way the school is organized and the other is the way the employees are dealt with. The amount of autonomy generally depends on the competency of the faculty and the amount of control the administrator believes is needed. Increased autonomy generally yields greater empowerment, but that isn't always the case. Teachers may be empowered through valuing their input, even if they don't have much independence.

Zero-tolerance policies, for instance, may both foster and undermine a teacher's sense of empowerment. If a teacher is supported by the administration for disciplining a high school student with behavioral problems, the teacher feels empowered. What teachers might consider is that seeking agreement for their beliefs or actions is a sure way to create splits and ultimately fractures among the faculty. It's a survival instinct for adversarial cultures, but in itself turns communication into a tool for climate decline. If a teacher is forced to witness a kindergarten student being suspended for bringing a nail clipper to school, without being consulted, they may feel disempowered.

CHAPTER 7

Infrastructure

Before a house can be built, there needs to be blueprints to help guide the construction. In those blueprints you will first find plans for the plumbing, the electrical circuitry, and the framing of each room. Beyond the physical layout you will find a crew that has a foreman who directs the order and method for building. You will also find supporting documents such as licenses and permits that regulate the parameters of the domicile. Even beyond those observable aspects of the construction will be the care of detail that goes into the work. Do the builders knowingly ignore design flaws that may be missed by the occupants or will they spend the extra time and money in creating a sound structure? These are some of the factors that create the infrastructure of the house. In an occupied building such as a school, we will find many of the same components.

The infrastructure of a school is the foundation or network of supporting structures responsible for daily operations. The infrastructure is composed of several components, including the policies/procedures, leadership, physical environment, espoused values, and integrity of the institution. Together, these components form a working picture of the organization so that others may know their role and expectations within. This picture also provides information for those being serviced by the organization. All five components of the school's infrastructure are born out of the mission and vision of the school, at least in theory, even if not specifically by the wording of these guiding principles, but certainly then by the school's attempt to be consistent between theory and practice of operation will the infrastructure be impacted.

The mission and vision of a school comprise the framework from which the daily operations flow. As is typical in most schools, however, the mission and vision are rarely utilized to the extent of shaping daily operations. How many faculty members actually know their school's mission/vision statements? This may be the case because schools do not often develop mission and vision statements that are reflective of the entire school culture. Instead, schools focus more on the product of their work as opposed to the process by which this end result is achieved. In most elementary and secondary schools, it is unlikely you will find reference to the faculty and their needs in this doctrine. Instead, there may be rhetoric about safe and healthy learning environments geared toward the student learner, but little that promotes well-being among the faculty.

Although administrators and teachers hold similar objectives for the school, there is oftentimes less agreement about the process by which these objectives are reached. If schools lack a shared picture around the process of operations, yet teachers are expected to follow and promote the organization's plan of action, friction may result. It is the school's leadership and not the faculty who derive these important philosophical standards, for instance, the mission/vision statement.

Since the mission and vision statements typically come from the leadership of the school and reflect those core values, both known and unknown, the risk is philosophical discord. While pragmatics may prevent each new teacher that enters a school to re-create the mission/vision, the teacher's orientation could include the start of dialogue between personal and organizational convergence. Even better, this process may begin during the interview and hiring process. Philosophical discord is a precursor to relational disharmony, creating greater fragmentation among the faculty and students.

Another problem is found when examining mission and vision statements created in the past that do not reflect either the current views of the administration or the changing society the school is embedded within. With the continuous turnover of school administrators, mission and vision statements may be ignored or discounted. If it is deemed important that teachers be exposed to these guiding principles early, then the same has to be said for the organizational leaders.

A similar pragmatic concern exists for school leadership as the position shifts occur with relative frequency. Superintendents, for instance, have an average tenure in their position of 3 years, creating an additional challenge to the school district. Either the new leader will revise the mission/vision statement or he or she will bring his or her own agenda that perhaps works contrary to these doctrines. Regardless, the behavior of the administrators will convey his or her attitudes and beliefs, which guide their work. Superintendents and principals, like every other manager, integrate their personal values in their work. These values may or may not resonate with those of the faculty, or the mission/vision, which is where dissonance is created. Furthermore, if a high percentage of the faculty does not know what the mission and vision of the school are, then a third variable of comparing their own personal beliefs comes into play. If this is the case, how can the faculty or administration be cognizant of how their own agenda fits with that of the organization they work for?

From the mission/vision springs forth policies and procedures of that school. A common mistake is for policies and procedures to be implemented without taking into consideration whether they are congruent with the guiding philosophy of that school when they may in fact be contrary. Policies and procedures offer guidelines for reward and discipline for both the faculty and the students. They include expectations for conduct and interaction among those within the school environment. Fair discipline practices and incentive guidelines create a sense of fairness, safety, and equity within that school's culture. When students feel safer they are less likely to resort to a more Darwinian approach to solving problems.

Leadership can be a force in creating the social energy that drives, or fails to drive, the organization. The way in which superintendents, principals, vice principals, and other leaders attend to their own relational styles will shape the school in potentially healthy or unhealthy ways. When school leadership recognizes the importance of the faculty and their attitude toward daily operations, there will be a greater sense of teacher empowerment, leading to a more positive school climate. This, in turn, will create more productive classrooms. This holds true in most school systems where teachers have the most direct impact on student learning, the schools chief product. The greater the awareness regarding this issue by the leadership, the greater the potential for actualizing the concept into practice.

Strong leadership can promote greater loyalty among the faculty, staff cohesion, and reciprocal feedback loops, which help the principal to build increased awareness. A leader can also be receptive to feedback and willing to incorporate the views of others into their decision making. The trust of the teachers comes from believing the principal cares about the individual needs of the faculty. When this happens, the health of a school will be vastly superior, because the climate will be strengthened.

The first step in improving organizational health may rest with the individual leader who engages in a process of self-exploration. Individual self-awareness can serve as a model for the entire school faculty. Understanding how the organization deals with change (adaptation), how conducive the environment is to work efficiently (climate), and the physical structure (infrastructure) in which daily operations spring from must all originate from this leadership.

FIVE KEY ASPECTS OF INFRASTRUCTURE

Leadership is a component of organizational culture insofar as the determination of organizational hierarchy, quality and quantity of supervision, allocation of power/control, and the level of autonomy is allocated to employees. The words, nonverbal messages, actions, and accomplishments of the leadership all come into play when shaping school culture. This is perhaps the reason why the quality of leadership is the greatest leading factor for job satisfaction in teacher surveys. With fervent attention to the symbolic side of their schools, leaders are said to assist in developing the foundation for change and success. Principals need to create the kind of environment where teachers can approach the leadership, to provide feedback and strategies that will create a better school environment.

Example A: You have worked at a school for 15 years under the same principal. This principal is well known for keeping his word and following through with every promise made. Because he takes his promises seriously, he is known for saying, "I'm not sure I can promise that, but I'll look into it and think about it." This is sometimes frustrating for the teachers who are eager for a quick solution. This principal is also well known for his open-door policy and makes sure each new teacher has his home phone and cell phone numbers. When an idea is brought to him and is implemented, he gives full credit to the person who has the idea.

Example B: You have worked at a school for 15 years under the same principal. This principal was very exciting to work for at first because he agreed to implement every new idea that was brought to him. It was quickly noticed that the ideas were rarely implemented. He is well known for saying "yes" and the teachers joke about how easily approval is given and how "no" is not in his vocabulary. His office hours are clearly posted, but rarely followed. If a teacher needs to speak with him, a meeting must be scheduled several days in advance through the secretary. He repeatedly says the teachers must make allowances for the last minute changes in meeting times "which are part of having my job." When an idea did get implemented, he would take full credit for the concept until something went wrong, in which case he would mention the name of the teacher who had the idea.

What do you see as the impact of these principals on the school culture? How do you suspect the leadership styles of these principals affect the teachers? The students? While the answers may not be entirely clear, beginning to consider the possibilities is an important step.

Policies and procedures are important determinants for organizational culture in that the rules and guidelines influence the attitudes and behavior of the employees and students. An organization may be described as employee friendly when policies and procedures are not rigid or stifling. When the policies support the mission of the school and have been well thought through, there is a greater clarity for the intentions of the school.

Example A: You are a newly hired teacher in a middle school with 400 students. Your principal requests input at a staff meeting regarding a new policy being discussed related to cell phones in the classrooms. The principal shares his concerns with you and your colleagues and relates information shared by principals in other schools within the district. Because the teachers are going to be the enforcers of this policy, the principal wants to make sure the teachers support the policy and have input about its implementation.

Example B: You are a newly hired teacher in a middle school with 400 students. Your principal makes an announcement during the last period that there will be a short staff meeting directly after school. At this meeting, the principal announces a new policy related to cell phones in the classrooms. Because the teachers are going to be the enforcers of this policy, the principal wants to make sure the teachers know the policy before it goes into effect on the next school day. The letter to the parents has already been mailed. A teacher raises a concern about the policy and is quickly told that the time for policy discussion is past—it is now written in stone.

While reading these examples, what did you feel? As a new teacher, which administrator would you feel better working with? What impact do you think the staff meeting would have on morale in Example A? Example B?

The *physical environment* will impact organizations in either a subtle or overt manner. A school with graffiti on the walls and video cameras on the ceilings will likely create a different atmosphere than hallways lined with the creative artwork from students. Many schools pay closer attention to the structural aspects of physical safety such as metal detectors and guards. While security personnel and equipment may heighten physical safety, this need is balanced with trust and privacy, which may be compromised by such measures. It has been found that the structure and layout of buildings or communities influence the attitudes and behaviors of the students.

Example A: A school has a large amount of money to invest in "school improvements" and the principal makes the unilateral decision to install cameras and other hall monitoring devices as well as new locks on the doors and reinforced windows on the first floor. While the changes feel secure they also create a prisonlike atmosphere. The principal assures the staff in the weekly meeting that these improvements will ensure the safety of the staff and the students. There is little discussion about how others perceive the changes.

Example B: A school has a large amount of money to invest in "school improvements" and the principal wants the end result to be a school that has an atmosphere conducive to learning as well as being safe. A meeting is held with representatives of the student government to hear their opinion about how the money should be spent. It is made clear that this is a preliminary meeting and no promises could be made at this stage. The student representatives share the concerns about the peeling paint in the classrooms and how the students feel they are attending school in "a dump," which is demoralizing. They also point to the 2-year decline in interest in the drama and music department and explain that this has been due to the problems with the stage lighting, the ripped curtain, and the missing floor tiles. Students feel that if the school doesn't care about the department, why should they. Money is set aside immediately for these improvements, which add up to only a small portion of the total budget.

How do you think the implementation of the improvements suggested by the student government would affect the school culture? How would the increased security systems impact the culture? If you were principal, what would you do?

Integrity is the measure of how well a school follows through with what it purports to be about. Those schools that claim to be about certain values or principals but act differently will find a higher level of mistrust, suspicion, and even resentment.

Example A: A school creates a bullying prevention program to address the increased number of complaints from parents. The program uses students who are trained in peaceful conflict resolution strategies to help others students in distress. While the program appears fundamentally sound, there is a glaring problem. Teachers feel overpowered by their principal and are fearful themselves of her criticism.

Example B: The same school creates a bullying prevention program that is first born out of a experiential learning component—a consultant comes to the school to work with the faculty over the course of a month, helping them to develop mechanisms among themselves to relate more effectively.

The *espoused values* are publicly announced principles from which the group claims to work. If a workplace has a lack of shared values or does not follow them consistently, employees may develop or implement their own belief system. Values oftentimes guide decision making where policies/procedures do not apply.

Example A: A school promotes on their website and throughout all printed publications that its students are treated with respect. The teachers are often heard yelling at the students and calling them names. One teacher is overheard by the principal saying to a student, "Don't be as dumb as your brother." Another is heard saying, "Is your hat on backwards because your brain is on backwards?" The principal does nothing about this, leaving the disciplining of the students to the teachers. When a parent complains to the principal, she is told the teachers need to have autonomy when it comes to discipline and they know best how to handle the students.

Example B: A school promotes on their website and throughout all printed publications that its students are treated with respect. The principal hears a teacher yelling at a student and saying, "Don't be as dumb as your brother." The principal calls the teacher in for a meeting and asks what precipitated the comment. The principal then reminds the teacher that the students are the "customer" in the school and deserve respect. The teacher is asked to give examples of other ways the situation could be handled and to put herself in the shoes of the student while thinking about it. The principal recognizes that the teacher is feeling overwhelmed with classroom discipline and is having some personal problems, which are affecting her mood at school. The principal asks in what way he can support the teacher.

Even though both examples show an initial breach of the espoused value, the second example shows the commitment of the school principal to prevent this as an ongoing problem. If the principal had scolded the teacher in front of the student, how would that impacted the culture? What was the biggest difference in the attitudes and behaviors of the two principals?

CHAPTER 8

An Integrated System

The organizational health of a school system is the combination of the three dimensions previously outlined. While adaptation, climate, and infrastructure are separate concepts, they are best understood if examined not in isolation, but in the way they are interrelated. The interaction of these three dimensions comprises the overall health of the organization and perhaps the success of that school system.

It is important to view schools within the context of an entire educational system when considering a measure of organizational health. Without viewing schools in this broad and bending manner, we miss out on valuable interaction effects, which seem to go unrecognized and therefore are not dealt with adequately.

Within this integration, we have outlined the importance to viewing organizational health on a continuum of polarities. A school may have tremendous consistency and predictability, yet these traits are born out of high structure, which can also be perceived as rigidity and inflexibility. Where a school views itself along various continuums influences how each of the three dimensions of organizational health interacts with the others. If we take, for instance, a school where teachers believe rigidity interferes with modernization, organizational health may be deemed poor. If we were to ask administration about the school's health, they may cite organization and consistency as their evidence for success. Perception, therefore, plays a major role in the determination of the degree to which organizational health is being achieved.

We have also described the difficulty school systems have measuring success in organizational health. While most schools may use some measure of student achievement, such as standardized test scores, report card grades, or, for high schools, the enrollment rate in college, high variability still exists. Those schools that are aware of the methods by which students become accomplished academically will reference student learning and the process by which this goal is accomplished, such as the development of a school culture that is conducive to challenge, creativity, stimulation, and reward.

Success is likely reflected by the mission and vision statements and perhaps the degree to which there is consensus about these guiding principals within the organization. The greater the accord between actions and beliefs, the more likely it is that staff will relate better to one another and the students they serve. The greater the accord the more immediate and present the focus of the faculty becomes. The improved predictability of a school helps faculty put aside their concerns about what will be and focus more on what is.

The result is improved relationships, as faculty no longer feel the need to divide into restrictive cliques to protect themselves. Improved relationships promote a climate of trust and openness, improving the atmosphere at different junctures throughout the semester. With an open and cohesive school climate, the organization's resiliency toward adversity will aid in adapting to internal and external pressures from the environment. This is how the three dimensions of organizational health overlap and influence each other.

In highly adaptive schools, a climate of trust and openness may be pervasive, influencing the role of the leadership, a facet of the school's infrastructure. It is also likely that the infrastructure, as the foundation for the organization, creates a strong impact on climate and adaptation. Take, for instance, a cohesive faculty who trust and support one another like a championship athletic team (climate). With a high level of commitment to their school, problem resolution will likely be quicker and less disruptive, thereby affecting the school's ability to adapt. Similarly, this faculty will be able to adjust policies and procedures according to their shared beliefs and values, a component of infrastructure.

Adaptation in large part is shaped by the school's infrastructure. How the school is organized will determine how it copes with both internal and external pressures and ultimately the quality and direction of the change process itself. Teachers often turn to their colleagues for guidance and support, and, therefore, faculties are informal problem-solving systems.

These subsystems can be highly influenced by a school's infrastructure, such as the rules and beliefs set forth by the school leadership. An otherwise simple decision such as the scheduling of teacher free periods has a significant affect on teacher socialization, which is where many of the day-to-day decisions within a school are often made. If teachers of the same grade are not able to spend their free time together, either because of their schedules or classroom locations, each teacher will learn to function more autonomously. Recall that with the idea of polarities and continua, autonomy might be a positive, such as self-sufficiency, but it can also be isolating and segregating.

Climate, in some part, resulting from the other two dimensions, is a key determinant in shaping a school's culture. The result of how this culture is shaped is what determines the school's overall health. Schools that are highly efficient due to a solid infrastructure, but lack the ability to adapt to external changes because of their rigidity, will have a climate marked by pressured and guarded relationships. This school's culture would incorporate the strengths and weaknesses of these three dimensions, the interactions of which would determine the overall health. If we were to observe how these dimensions interrelate, we might find a leadership that that does not promote creativity and autonomy. This in turn may lower teacher efficacy, influencing the willingness of the faculty to extend themselves in extracurricular activities for the students. The circular dynamics will continue endlessly unless the system is able and willing to scan their environment, thereby increasing the awareness of the inherent patterns within the system.

Returning to the original definition of organizational health, we note an organization's awareness of the three dimensions of culture and how these dimensions interdependently influence one another. Without one clearly identified and agreed upon definition of organizational health and because of the discrepancy between what defines health across an extreme diversity of schools themselves, awareness remains the key determinant of whether a school can effectively improve. With an increased awareness of the complexity within that system, there will be an increased potential to re-create or reshape the system to better meet the organization's particular needs.

None of the areas for improved school health addressed within this book are new, nor are they complicated in nature. In fact, many schools are already addressing many of these issues in their own manner. Rather than mystifying the process with sophisticated jargon, the intent is for schools to recognize the enormity of these tasks (integrating the three dimensions) when it comes to application. Schools, like other organizations, are not accustomed to exploring these rather basic concepts because of limited time and energy. Similar to your personal health, organizational health is often ignored until there is a problem. Without continuous attention to how the organization is experiencing the unrelenting currents of change and sameness, the institution risks becoming mired in bureaucracy, which interferes with fluid operations.

While improving school health will not compensate for factors such as inadequate resources, low teacher salaries, single parent/low income families, neighborhood deterioration, and so on, it will help schools cope more successfully with the effects of these impediments to success. Without a process for attending to the impact of these factors, schools will become increasingly helpless to provide a quality education for the children who will eventually deal with these societal ills. The most extreme result of a school that does not scan itself having lesser awareness is a climate of guardedness and hostility.

Part III

ORGANIZATIONAL HEALTH AND STUDENT VIOLENCE

CHAPTER 9

Organizational Violence

Violence in the workplace is a more commonly used expression for this most recent categorization of aggression. Previous estimates have put homicide as the second leading cause of death in the workplace.

To understand the dynamics of organizational violence, we need to go beyond the surface and through the many layers of complexity that breed this antisocial explosion. A comparison to volcanoes will be used to illustrate this phenomenon. With volcanoes, our focus is generally drawn to the eruption itself, instead of the underlying dynamics responsible for this event. So too with violence, we often attend to the aggressive act without truly understanding the build-up to this event. If we want to reduce the potential for violence in our organization, we first attend to the process from which violence begins. To do so, we can look at the geological stages of a volcano.

In order for a volcano to erupt, a number of specific conditions must be met. The large plates that divide the earth must be aligned in such a way as to produce friction on their boundaries. The resulting heat and pressure causes the mantle to melt into magma. When enough magma is formed, it rises through the denser rock layers toward the earth's surface, creating what is called a subversion eruption.

Such a comparison can be made to organizational violence. Conditions are similar in that a number of subsystems, instead of plates, come together forming friction. This friction may be the result of decision making, group formation, boundary shifts, power struggles, and other poiitic events. The resulting pressure experienced individually and within groups may lead to competition, hurt feelings, rejection, isolation, and the overall deterioration of a person's resiliency. If this pattern is continuous, a person can becomes hopeless, experiences a sense of powerlessness, and ultimately lashes out.

There are different types of volcanic eruptions. A nonexplosive eruption may occur with effusive lava flow. This is comparable to the more subtle expression of violence found in harassment, bullying, social isolation, self-mutilation, and other forms of self-harm.

An explosive eruption with voluminous lava flow is synchronistic with volatile acts of aggression such as violent and catastrophic assault. The complexity of the volcanic eruption is similar to that of violence perpetrated by adults, in that it is difficult to predict. Scientists who study volcanoes are aware, however, that one factor or set of factors is not sufficient for the understanding of the eruption process. They appreciate the subtle and overt factors that play a role, even though they may be more difficult to measure, such as plate shifting.

Predicting violence is often as difficult, but the key lies in understanding the complexity of events, not in rushing to scapegoat or blame any one factor. We can begin this understanding by examining the clues we have been presented with. With a volcano we measure the amount of magma accumulating in reservoirs, watching as the gases come closer to the surface. We may sometimes experience earthquakes or vibrations warning that an eruption may be eminent. To recognize this process we use tools such as seismographs and correlation spectrometers. These tools help gather data that improve the estimates for impending disaster.

With respect to organizational violence, some experts who study institutions of education suggest that we don't often monitor the process nor do we always look for the clues. Some experts suggest that we monitor the at-risk children who may be predisposed to committing such events. Unfortunately, this is only the tip of the mountain, as the process begins deep below the surface. The tools for monitoring this process are our own self- and systems-awareness, regularly discussed by all those who are involved in sustaining the organization.

As with a seismograph, the faculty must monitor the spikes in tension experienced at different intervals throughout the school year. Attention to various internal and external pressures needs to be brought into the public forum so that decisions can be made on how to release the tension. Oftentimes the act of open dialogue alone is enough to reduce the tension if the process is fluid and finds closure. If the process is stagnated in some way, it can actually create more friction than no intervention at all.

Organizations that do not take responsibility for exploring the impact of their environment can be viewed as coconspirators in many violent episodes. The term systemic violence has been used to describe aggressive acts that take place within an institution and are typically promoted by factors experienced within. While they might recoil at the suggestion that their school might be implicated in the violent acts of students, educators must try to avoid the instinct to defend. The intention is not to lay blame but instead to look for the role of the system. Organizational leaders who fear public stigmatization will be surprised to find the welcome reception they receive from a public who seeks understanding and not blame.

CHAPTER 10

Existing Prevention Programs

The impact of widespread media attention has lead to two major changes within the educational system in how we deal with youth violence and the prevention thereof. The first major change is the implementation of new programs, such as character education, peer mediation, and antibullying programs. The second change is the advent of stricter punitive measures for student aggression. Neither of these changes alone is sufficient for dealing with reducing the potential for violence. It can be argued that these interventions might actually increase the potential for violence.

While building morals and values through character education is helpful, it will be perceived as an empty gesture by children and teachers, who do not experience these same principles throughout the school. Bullying prevention programs certainly have a place in our educational institutions, but the root of bullying can only be found by digging under the surface of youth aggression. In schools where teachers feel a lack of support from administration or even view their principal as hostile, bullying prevention programs will ultimately prove hypocritical.

Stricter punitive measures as a deterrent for youth aggression has the risk of reinforcing aggression and scapegoating perpetrators. While on some level, fear of consequences may serve as an inhibitor to violence, no amount of fear will stop a child who feels ostracized on a daily basis and seeks retaliation against his or her peers. The two perpetrators of the Columbine massacre are examples of this, as their intended plan was slaughter followed by suicide. If we make a scapegoat of youth who commit violent acts, we are redirecting the problem from the culture in which violence became an acceptable means of problem solving.

In existing violence prevention programs, skill building focuses on deficits found in violent adolescents and adults, such as a lack of empathy, impulse control, problem solving, and anger management. Anyone spending time in a teachers' lounge can find these similar deficits. Albeit these deficits present in a milder form, the constant barrage of complaints about administration resemble a lack of empathy, impulse control, and problem-solving skills. Faculty who experience resentment or mistrust toward their administration may not seek to fully understand the constraints and limitations of the school system. Instead they feel powerless, in part due to their own lack of problem-solving skills. Reflexively or impulsively, they make independent decisions that are geared toward self-preservation, rather than the best interest of the team or school itself.

It isn't surprising, however, that existing violence prevention programs are geared toward skill building because it reflects the recommendations in educational reform literature. Prevention efforts are heavily geared toward conflict resolution and peer mediation, with uncertainty whether these strategies will address the underlying tension that gave rise to interpersonal violence.

An important determinant in the success or failure of any prevention program is the amount of ownership by the faculty. Without the support of the entire school staff, new programs will not be implemented. A belief in the prevention efforts by the faculty will either serve as an inspiriting factor for the students or a deterrent. Therefore, faculty who are involved in the decision-making process of selecting a prevention approach, or are at least kept well informed of the decision-making process, will be more likely to approach these efforts with greater receptivity.

Since schools are hierarchically designed, as discussed earlier, they frequently leave such decisions to the administrators. In these cases it is important to recognize that support for prevention programs may come more slowly due to increased resistance. Faculty may believe their input around decisions directly affecting them has less importance and they will therefore be less willing to participate or may overtly or covertly sabotage implementation.

Teaching tolerance is a primary tool for existing prevention programs. During a developmental stage in which acceptance is the main goal for adolescents, similarities emerge as the unifying force between peers. Similarly, differences are perceived as threatening and oftentimes dealt with through ostracism and even aggression. Tolerance, however, is learned best when it is experiential and not didactic. Students learn tolerance as well through the modeling of adults in their lives. Faculty who are not aware of their own biases and prejudices toward students and each other will unconsciously influence students in a similar direction.

Certain prevention programs suggest that a core team of personnel be trained within the school district to learn about, implement, and monitor school efforts. This is an interesting approach to have a core team be primarily responsible for violence prevention. While it may be more efficient and practical to train a portion of the faculty, those members not involved in the training will be less inspired to implement the approach. A potential drawback of creating this support team is further fragmentation of the faculty. If the school culture is mired in cliques among the faculty, then promoting further hierarchical structures could prove to reinforce the dynamic of dissension.

There is a significant distinction between skill building and transformational change. While most prevention programs put their faith in the acquisition of new tools for problem solving, such as anger management, appreciating diversity, and impulse control, a whole system approach recognizes the limitations of this design. Analogous to this situation is the medical intervention of treating a person suffering from a chronic illness by rehydrating them. While the patient may in fact feel better for the time being, without addressing nutrition, exercise, stress management, and other patterns of living, the immune system will become overwhelmed repeatedly.

Utilizing a systems approach to understanding and working with school violence has its own set of challenges. It requires a deeper level of commitment on the part of the administration and faculty, which involves more time, energy, and money, all of which are in short supply in most schools. The complexity of making changes on an organization level is not easy, which is another consideration for perspective schools. As it has been proposed, individualized change is complicated in itself, so changing multiple levels of a system is inherently more complex. The reasons against this type of undertaking are more apparent on the surface than the possible outcomes of this work.

If we don't utilize a contextual approach to school violence, we are requesting the subsystem with the least power and control—the students—to be the ones to make the greatest change.

Even with the argument made in favor of a more contextual approach to reducing student violence, the argument will continue to be made that violence prevention programs are designed to improve peer relationships and thereby reduce the impact of gangs, bullying, and other acts of violence. Remember, however, that simply creating these programs within a larger milieu that remains unchanged is not only ineffectual but also hypocritically damaging. It is analogous to a parent being abused by his or her spouse and telling his or her child that hitting a sibling is wrong.

Prevention programs need to be further inclusive of the environment in which they are implemented. In order for schools to consider broadening their perspective of the powerful forces that impact student violence, data must be collected that support the position of understanding school culture. Research that incorporates potentially influential systemic factors that influence student violence can help with this endeavor.

CHAPTER 11

School Culture and Student Violence

There is overwhelming evidence to support the premise that school culture affects the level of violence among students. When a culture becomes so toxic that staff feel fragmented, teaching feels overly burdensome, and as hopelessness sets in, the potential for violence rises. While there may be strong resistance to the conclusion that schools play a major role in the potential for student violence, this reality can no longer be avoided.

School culture should be considered not simply a causative factor for the aggressive behavior of students, but more like a set of correlative variables that have yet to be validated empirically and gain support in public perception. The media is responsible for perpetuating the externalization of blame that has served to protect schools while in fact making them more vulnerable.

School administrators do not always recognize or at least acknowledge the school's role in perpetuating student violence and therefore make insufficient effort to address how the system influences its potential. Instead, administrators as a whole seem to externalize responsibility for the aggressive acts by students onto the pupils themselves, their families, and society as a whole.

If school administrators diminish the school's role in perpetuating school violence, there needs to be reason for their lack of culpability. One such reason is that school officials may fear their schools will become stigmatized as unsafe if the issue of culture or organizational health is openly addressed. If administrators are fearful of public perception, their fear may influence how prevention efforts are directed. For example, a school leader may devote resources to prevention programs, pupil assessment strategies (violence poten-tial), and heightened security. Little attention, however, would be given to the school culture where students spend up to half of their waking hours, the same area that possesses the greatest potential to positively impact children during this vitally important developmen-tal period.

The speculation that administrators can alter their views about student violence due to public perception is difficult to support. While it may be safe to assume that administrators are concerned with the public and how it views their school, they may not go so far as to purposely curtail the appropriate steps for adequate vio-lence prevention. They may, however, not be fully aware of their motivation, as decisions are sometimes made more unconsciously. In the case of school administrators, the fear of stigmatization may play an underestimated role in decision making. Fear is a powerful motivator that is not often acknowledged openly because it suggests weakness. If administrators are fearful of identifying issues or or-ganizational culture within their schools, of which they have only a partial understanding, they may minimize the importance of this complex factor.

If administrators assume a passive role or take actions that are not comprehensive in scope, violence may in fact be enabled. Is it pos-sible that teachers are more aware of or at least willing to attribute causes for violence to the school system itself? Teachers, similar to other front line employees of an organization, are affected by their school's culture in similar ways as are the students, and therefore may be more aware of this impact. Bill Hardy (as cited in Henry, 1994), former president of the American Federation of Teachers, supported this premise when he suggested that principals don't re-port the full extent of violence because they fear the negative impact it might have on their own performance.

Teachers, however, are not always in a position of making deter-minations of how school systems address the problems of school vi-olence. Teachers, similar to the employees of any typical organizational workplace, do not view themselves to be in positions of power or influence regarding organizational dynamics.

Although teachers may be more aware of cultural influences because their experience is more similar to that of the students, they may not recognize the impact or know what to do about it. It is also possible that teachers will rationalize student aggression as socially sanctioned behavior that is out of their control, thus serving to normalize the behavior.

If teachers and administrators have differing beliefs regarding the causes of student violence, this discrepancy itself may affect the climate of the school. Differing perspectives on the causes of school violence might lead to situations where teachers do not feel supported by the administration with regard to discipline. In these instances, teachers may refrain from applying limits and other necessary disciplinary measures, leading to unsafe feelings in the students and dismay in school administrators.

Broadening this concept to include other differences between teachers and administration may yield important information on school culture. While culture itself may not be a causative factor of student violence, the positive or negative experience of that culture may in fact contribute to student aggression. If teachers and administrators have disrupted communication patterns and use inadequate processes for making decisions, or if there is general discontent among the faculty, organizational breakdown is likely to occur. When breakdown results, a survival of the fittest mentality may ensue, creating hierarchical power-influenced relating.

Poor job dissatisfaction, high faculty turnover, frequent conflict among faculty, and a rise in student behavioral problems are all examples of cultural influences that can begin a downward spiral. School systems that fail to explore, interpret, and act upon their internal cultural influences, such as tension among the faculty, are more likely to be vulnerable to student violence.

Students, influenced by their own need for safety, will likely experience the tensions created by the faculty either consciously or unconsciously. Similar to a child who grows up in a home where continual conflict exists between the parents, uncertainty and trepidation may develop. If the climate among faculty seems adversarial or even fragmented, often the result of administrative-faculty relations, students may feel unsafe. When children do not feel safe, some will utilize their own compensatory mechanisms such as bullying, intimidation, and dominance among themselves. Those with power will feel comforted by the control they usurp, while others will move toward the bottom of the pecking order.

While attitude does not equate to behavior, we many speculate that students will inevitably act upon their attitudes and beliefs about their perceptions regarding their school's culture. For instance, if teachers exude hostility or antipathy within a school, it may lead to decreased investment in the creation of a learning environment conducive to safety. While these cause and effect relations are difficult to validate, the possibility alone that teacher-administrator relations and other working conditions can contribute to a school's violence potential warrants further consideration.

While administrators and teachers may differ in their perceptions of their schools' cultural impact on student violence, current efforts to address this problem are largely insufficient. The media's coverage following each of the major violent episodes, such as those at Columbine and Little Rock, presented glaring similar messages to address this issue. When interviewed, experts on violence suggest that schools need to provide better prevention programs, do a better job assessing for violence potential among students, and also reach out to families where violence is bred. This approach veers attention away from the school, which is a more inviting strategy to communities as a whole.

Student violence will remain a complex phenomenon, one which simple solutions targeted in one specific area will not thoroughly or adequately address. Although we may not as a society experience an increase in systemic violence, we are seeing more catastrophic episodes of violent expression.

Without the tools to live and work with in the pressure-filled environment of the various forms of school culture, we will likely witness a continuation of this new trend in violent self-expression. Rather than extending our vast resources into programs aimed at building skills for our students to cope in their environment, we must work with the environment itself.

The school community, like every other organization, is a system much like a family; and addressing the system's needs requires us to understand the roles, boundaries, communication, and decision-making styles of that system. If we can better understand the systemic influence of the complex culture that makes up our school environments, we can work to create a milieu that is conducive to both learning and safety. To do this requires the willingness and openness of school administrators who are not driven solely by fear of disapproval. If administrators are receptive to this challenge, they will have already begun modeling that acceptance is not the only need to be satisfied in life.

CHAPTER 12

A Whole School Approach

A whole school approach means that the focus of violence prevention is broader yet more specific. Instead of targeting the students as the sole cause of aggression, we expand our thinking to include the entire system and each subsystem including parents, school boards, administrators, legislators, faculty, and the students, as well as the interrelatedness of each of these parts to form the whole. But before we begin to design such an approach, we need to examine the resistance, the obstacles to transforming our approach to violence prevention. We need to examine the challenges to making this paradigm shift unless we serve to strengthen the forces for sameness.

WHAT ARE THE OBSTACLES?

We find at least several major obstacles to utilizing a whole school approach for violence prevention. First, it is a financial issue that limits the acquisition of resources needed to comprehensively address this complex issue. Associated with financial limitation are the restrictions of time for the administrators. Unable to free themselves of the clerical and administrative obligations of their jobs, school leaders are not in a position to spend as much time with supervision, collaboration, and introspection as is needed to effectively manage their school culture. There are likely few principals who wouldn't want to be freed up to spend more energy dealing with the organizational health of their schools.

Second, it is an issue of politics. In local politics, it is the local school boards who create and review policies and procedures that influence the behaviors of school leaders. If the school board is un-involved or worse, it can influence the direction of the school, biased by its own self-interest or personal gain, and power struggles are then created.

On a regional or national level, lawmakers create legislation that is intended to help large geographic regions, not always taking into account the individual variability and uniqueness of each district. The Safe Schools Act is a good example of legislation that is de-signed to make schools safer; however, it also serves to reinforce the scapegoat mentality that puts blame on the individual child. Admin-istrators are now concerned that if parents were to suspect their school was "unsafe" they would request their child be sent to another school, which the district would have to pay for. By bringing atten-tion to the school culture, even as a mechanism to improve organi-zational health, the fear is public stigmatization.

Another major obstacle for schools to navigate is the stigma they perceive is associated with linking student violence to school cul-ture. Administrators from all over the country get anxious when we begin to associate the organizational health of their school with the potential for student violence. It is not that they don't believe this is a possibility, in fact most of them are well aware of the connection, it is more about the perception of the public, the media, their school district, and the legislators, all of whom influence their future as an administrator.

If principals open their schools to scrutiny, those in power who are less understanding of organizational dynamics or unimpressed with the individual principal's receptivity to improving school culture and thus look upon the principal unfavorably run the risk of jeopardizing their careers.

Not yet discussed is the perceived threat of judgment or evalua-tion by outside sources. Transforming a school culture is a compli-cated job, one that is aided by the support of an outside consultant that can offer an objective lens and a collaborative approach to sup-porting what is working while helping raise the awareness of the limitations of that approach.

And lastly, it is a matter of willingness on the part of school faculty and parents to take on this sizable challenge. Is this going to be another burdensome change that will be viewed as short-lived and an extraordinary waste of time/energy? Any veteran teacher who has been around for some time will tell you about the numerous changes that were supposed to revolutionize education, only to be replaced by a new paradigm. Transformational change takes a full commitment on the part of the entire school community.

There are many variables outside of our control that factor into the proclivity for student violence. Family influences, such as domestic violence and child abuse, poverty, and the lack of positive resources for our children; the media and its glorification of violence; and numerous other external factors to the school culture play a role in the tendency to act violently. We cannot control these influences any more than we can fix the mental health issues that predispose a child to act violently. We can continue to put energy into building supports for these children who are at risk, and we ought to do so. There is a lack of trained professionals who are available to counsel children who can very easily turn to drugs, gangs, cults, and other harmful influences.

Ask any psychologist or social worker who works on a Native American reservation what his or her caseload is and you will learn that these job have become reactive, putting out fires and doing crisis management. Or check with (inner-city) school counselors, who are rationed one per four schools, and ask them to make time for all the children who need them. The bottom line is our schools are underfunded and the staff are becoming increasingly burdened with intrapersonal problems beyond the scope of their time and often their training. Again, many of these factors are outside our control, so we must focus our energy on those dynamics that are within our sphere of influence.

WHAT ARE THE BENEFITS?

If we can first move away from the temptation to blame the disturbed child, the one whom the media portray as a bad seed or the ticking time bomb, then we might be more willing to examine variables that *are* within our control. Indeed although the teenager in Red Lake, Minnesota, who killed nine students and faculty injuring seven others, experienced terrible tragedies throughout his life—the suicide of his father, the car accident resulting in permanent brain damage and subsequent nursing care for his mother—there is much more to his rampage that familial turmoil.

If we look deeper we will find a young man who didn't fit in with his peer group so he did what many teens his age do—find an alternative method of affiliation. Initial reports indicate an affinity for nazi beliefs, which may have helped him to feel a part of some group. For teenagers this is the most significant developmental task, and if it doesn't happen the conventional way, through school friendships, then more significant turmoil will likely yield more serious problems. Whether the child implodes, through depression or anxiety, or explodes, through violence or other behavioral problems, we cannot always predict the outcome of this lack of social integration.

If we listen to the news reports, in particular the interviews with the "experts," we hear commentary on "the dangers of Prozac" or that the teen was "deeply troubled." These are the news headlines that followed the massacre at Columbine as well. There were other opinions, however, that looked beyond the obvious, exploring some of the social and contextual factors that likely played a role.

One such anonymous quote came from the website TalkLeft: The Politics of Crime (talkleft.com). In this threaded discussion, a reader was quoted as saying:

> I hope the media coverage won't ignore the culture of intolerance that exists at these schools, and that it is a factor that has existed with most school shootings: the shooters were taunted/ridiculed and made to feel like outsiders and outcasts. Our schools should be developing zero-tolerance policies for students who practice the politics of exclusion.

While punishment for ostracism is not likely to work, mainly because it's a fairly natural social phenomenon, which is likely occurring to some degree within the faculty as well, the notion is that other factors outside the intrapersonal dynamics of the teen him- or herself were responsible for the aggression. If the young man was being harassed or bullied by his peers, how did the school handle it? Was it a known and accepted practice within the school? The community? What led the children within the school to behave in this way, such as the organizational health of the school? If we can expand our exploration beyond the perpetrator, without blaming the school for this catastrophe, we will find valuable information to help us begin designing prevention strategies.

In speaking with educators across the country, it seems that there are ways to better anticipate student aggression, in fact there are even ways to decrease the potential that violence will happen in your school: by improving communication and teamwork, by better following through with policies and procedures that are fair and balanced, by improving the morale of the faculty so that teachers take the time needed to reach out to those students at risk, and by strengthening the leadership that sets the tone for organization and accountability. In other words, by building a stronger school culture that promotes greater organizational health, we can decrease the likelihood that students will feel abandoned and excluded within the school environment.

Improving organizational heath is similar to improving your own personal health, except there are more subsystems over which you have less control. If you continue to get colds and your physician advises you to take better care of yourself, what do you do? You might start by improving your nutrition, taking vitamins, adding in some exercise, and if you're really ambitious, taking a vacation from your stress. If necessary, you might be encouraged to visit a nutritionist, get a massage, or sign up for a yoga class.

Instead of one particular strategy or recommendation that will improve our health, there are multiple factors—psychological, emotional, behavioral, relational, and physiological—that play a role. In fact, it is oftentimes a combination and interaction of these factors that ultimately determine a person's health.

Organizational health is also a combination and interaction of factors, though few schools have been presented with comprehensive information on what those factors are and how they are interconnected. Even with this information it is difficult to determine in what way this information can be utilized to improve the health of the organization and ultimately reduce the potential for student violence. Because this work is so complicated and time- and energy-consuming, we can be tempted by simpler "solutions."

We know there is no single answer. Instead we are in need of a reorganization of perception about the problem itself and the solution. If we can reframe the issue from our current scapegoats, including families, poverty, media, and so forth, into a broader systemic view of multiple causalities we may have a chance at successfully addressing the violence potential of each school.

The first belief to be addressed is that violence happens outside the scope and influence of the school system. Administrators and teachers will need to accept the idea that the health of the school system is largely dependent upon the culture created within that school, and thus culture is the biggest controllable factor in a school's violence potential. The attitude of externalizing blame and finding scapegoats must change in order for all invested parties to increase their awareness of the systemic influences of home, school, and community. With this attitude comes the behavior of quick-fix solutions by schools because administrators are fearful of being thought of as inadequate or incapable of protecting their children.

As a community, school, or classroom leader, you can be a pioneer in the transformation of your school's culture. If you will begin conversations with other teachers, politicians, parents, and educators about the role of school culture, you can begin to alter the stigma that prevents attention from being shifted toward this area. Since schools are relatively closed systems that are easily threatened by outside forces, these conversations may be most effective if they begin within the school, so you are not perceived as a threat yourself. If you are a teacher, you can model this for your administrators by having conversations within the classroom. The process begins when you create a culture conducive to learning within your four walls and down your corridors.

If you are a superintendent or school board member, you can reward those principals who risk scrutiny by addressing these aspects of organizational health. It is the ambitious leader with equal regard for self and institution who will put his or her professional reputation at stake; and there is no other way to address organizational health in this day and age without doing so. As soon as the school leader opens the door to evaluation, a prerequisite for strengthening the culture, the risk of outside prejudice grows. Instead of waiting to see what the result of this self-examination is, superintendents and school boards can put their full support behind their principal. Putting politics aside temporarily will yield valuable gains in the long run.

When urging schools to utilize a whole school approach to violence prevention, it is important to recognize the limited resources and support a school may receive to implement these ideological and pragmatic changes. And without adequate funding, training, time, or support to move in this direction, the quick fix solution becomes more attractive, as it appears the schools are taking violence prevention seriously. Ideally, a school would bring in an outside consultant who can help the faculty reduce their blind spots.

USING A CONSULTANT

If the fear of stigmatization was high in acknowledging the role of school culture in student violence, consider the terror of bringing in a consultant. It doesn't usually help to know that high-powered executives from Fortune 500 companies spend tens of thousands of dollars to have this outside assistance, because schools are organizations unlike any other. In the eyes of most administrators, seeking help outside the district is tantamount to admitting defeat. They believe they will be replaced in their jobs if they are viewed as unable to handle management themselves.

With all that said, hiring a consultant can be the most important part of organizational transformation. Similar to a person who finally makes the decision to seek therapy, the willingness to get help can be a huge relief. This is mainly because we are not able to see all that needs to be seen when we are working alone, which makes the objectivity of a consultant invaluable. In addition to this objective viewpoint, a consultant offers expertise in organizational dynamics, including executive coaching, employee development, staff relations, and team building, to name just a few methods of assistance. Because this is still a risky venture, there is an actual dialogue that can help one understand the consulting process from start to finish.

Consider the following dialogue between a consultant and a school principal to illustrate some of the ways resistance is dealt with. This principal of this school brought in a consultant upon the request of the school superintendent following an episode of violence within the school. The consultant, knowing he was perceived as a threat, attempts to gain acceptance.

"You are not happy with having an outsider come into your school, it sounds."

She was surprised by his directness and that he chose to focus on her instead of the incident she just described.

"Well no I wouldn't say that I was unhappy, it's just that I don't know what it is you can really do for us."

Dr. Fanning considered that for a moment and then said, "It may seem intrusive for an outsider to come into your school, especially when it is not by your choice entirely and when you don't even know how or if it can be helpful. And this coming so soon after such a serious trauma."

He was very good, she thought to herself, and it didn't seem at all like an act. He genuinely understood her dilemma, which helped put her at ease.

"Believe me," he continued, "I am not here to find fault with the school or disrupt your hard work. The last thing I imagine you would need now is more pressure on you or the school."

"We are under a lot of pressure. Still I don't know if that is a reason to bring in a consultant. I have never heard of this except in cases where the school district is having serious financial problems and an expert comes in to cut costs."

"You are right, it is not altogether common for a school to utilize a consultant, but that is most unfortunate."

"Why is that?" she asked.

"Well, consultants have only become popular in the past 10 years, used most commonly in large organizations. CEOs hire consultants when there is a significant disruption in the company, such as a merger or a change in leadership. I believe there is a greater recognition that consultants can help improve productivity, efficiency, and even produce long-term financial savings. Sometimes consultants are called upon when a crisis has occurred and there is urgency to fix a serious problem. Schools, however, which turn out the most important product in the world, rarely consider using the services of a consultant."

Mrs. Smith wasn't sure what to make of this analogy, as she had never considered learning to be a product.

"We don't really have problems with efficiency here, we keep a pretty tight ship."

"I would suspect that your school is highly organized and efficient. A consultant's job as I see it is not to find fault, but to build on existing strengths. Even highly efficient systems can find room for growth, but only when there is a heightening of awareness about how you operate."

He could see that Mrs. Smith did not fully comprehend his meaning.

"Let me describe it this way. A family such as the one here at your school is working toward improvements in many areas each day. Learning new teaching methods, implementing state and federal guidelines, and developing more effective behavior modification. Before making changes to each anticipated goal, you must have a clear picture of what are presently strengths or weaknesses. When you use awareness as a tool for improvement, you generally find your strengths and their inherent deficits."

"What do you mean?" she meant to think to herself but said out loud.

"Let's look at this process on an individual level. We can use myself as an example. I view myself as fairly persistent. When it comes to tasks I am not quite skilled in, such as fixing an electrical problem, I don't easily give up, sometimes spending more time and effort than it is worth. So this seemingly useful character trait can have its drawback. Another way of looking at it is perspective. I might say perseverance, while my wife might view me as stubborn."

Mrs. Smith smiled at the example.

"A strength to one person can be perceived as a weakness to another, based on his or her own life experiences, needs, conflicts."

Mrs. Smith wondered about the relevance to her school.

"I'm not sure how all this applies to us. We are a school without too many problems and we had what I consider an extraordinary occurrence. The way I think you might be helpful to us is to improve our peer mediation program. We just set this up recently, and I'm sure it can stand some improvement."

Dr. Fanning was aware in the obvious shift in focus and became slightly impatient.

"While I like any programs designed for children to feel empowered, I don't believe peer mediation programs by themselves are a solution to violence," he replied.

"You look surprised," he said, "let me clarify myself. Having a system where children help each other resolve problems is very positive. In my experience it is meaningless, however, without addressing the underlying issues that create the need for this program in the first place."

Her surprised look turned to skepticism.

"Are you saying that the school caused this young man to act with utter disregard for another person's life?"

"You don't have to have overt problems within a system for events such as violence to occur. An undercurrent of tension exists in every institution where people work together. Sometimes that tension spikes, and if conditions exist to spark this tension, aggression can occur. The idea is to become aware of the tension and how to work with it, so that it does not influence people toward implosion or explosion. Let me stop for a moment because I think I got into a bit more than I intended to on our first meeting. I want you to understand that I am not here to give advice on programs and that I don't want to give any direct causation to the events of last month. My goal for you would not be to uncover problems within your school that led to violence, but more to help the school reach a more satisfying state of functioning that better serves the staff and students. If this state an be attained, there may be a lessening of potential for student violence and certainly a process to heal from this trauma."

"The truth of it is, Dr. Fanning, that we had a rare violent act by a single student that will probably never happen again," Ms. Smith replied.

"The truth about student violence, Mrs. Smith, is that it is misunderstood. I too hope that it will never occur here again, but you may consider this event to be a warning and not just a misfortunate outcome."

"To be honest," Mrs. Smith began, "this is not at all what I expected." I think I can understand your philosophy, but I am not sure if we are ready for all that."

"I know that it must sound overwhelming. Perhaps you can tell me a little more about what you would like to see happen in your school?"

"I'm not sure I understand your question," replied Mrs. Smith.

"If you were to bring in a consultant on your own terms to help you with any change effort within your school, what would it be?"

Mrs. Smith needed to think about this question. She considered herself more of a pragmatist, working with what she had instead of wishing for something different.

"Well, I suppose there are small things that could stand improvement, but I think we can just as easily go on without them."

"What would that be?" asked Dr. Fanning.

"I would want greater investment by the teachers, less conflict among the faculty—it is very disruptive to our daily operations— higher test scores by the children, and more involvement from the parents. And it goes without saying that I want a safe environment where events such as the one from last month do not happen."

Dr. Fanning nodded vehemently.

"Those sound like remarkable goals. I would estimate that the work needed to address all these goals can be done simultaneously, including the reduction in student violence."

"You said violence of the students," interrupted Mrs. Smith. "We don't have a violence problem, it was only that one incident."

"Well, I think this may reflect a larger issue, which is how I conceptualize violence on the whole. I don't think a school needs to have multiple episodes of aggression to have a violence problem. I see violence as a sociological epidemic that is spreading across this country and even the world. We all live the consequences of it, but only some of us have the opportunity to make a difference. I view schools as the key in this new era to making that significant difference."

"How are schools supposed to make a difference? I don't mean to sound skeptical, but as a whole we are more affected by student violence than any other group as a whole."

"This is true. It is also the case that schools are the only place aside from the home, which exerts a steady and constant influence upon the child. While at this point in time we are inadvertently feeding the problem, years from now I hope we can be part of the solution."

"How are we part of the problem? We have developed zero-tolerance policies, making a clear statement to anybody committing this sort of act that it will not be acceptable. Do you think this kind of policy is wrong?"

"I believe that higher standards are well intentioned, but not in and of themselves effective. Take the state and federal standards imposed on the schools for academic progress. While the goal is to raise performance, I believe there are many who would consider this unreasonable. They would likely say we are hearing the what but not getting the how."

Mrs. Smith considered this for a moment while Dr. Fanning went on.

"In the year 2000, Congress debated goals for future legislation. They already had content and performance standards, so it was suggested they add a third one called opportunity to learn standards. I believe this was the closest anybody has come to recognizing the missing piece. You can certainly legislate the what, yet this was an attempt to question the how."

"What would your suggestion to Congress be?"

"I would have wanted the third standard to be the how or more precisely the process. We know what we want to attain, so we may consider the way in which this can be done. Take violence reduction for instance. We may agree that a reduction in violent episodes are desired, but are not in agreement about the best means to accomplish this goal."

"Is there a best way to do this?" asked Mrs. Smith.

"I believe there is no one right way. This is both the problem and the solution. We must recognize what works in Butte, Montana, may be different from Jamaica, Queens. The way we arrive at these answers can be similar. If we pay attention to how we ask the questions and come up with the answers, we can create a higher-level self-regulating system. We can create school environments where the importance is now the way in which we solve problems and not the problems themselves. And isn't that what we want to teach our children? It's not just what they are learning but the process of thinking and deciding for themselves. We don't want automatons coming out of our schools that can simply recite the formulas for mathematical equations; we want children who can understand the reasoning behind the formula. We don't just want children who understand that a world war took place on this particular date, we want them to question why wars happen in the first place.

"Violence is not simply the problem, it is the result of many problems gone unanswered. We can't eliminate aggression simply because it is damaging. We must first understand the factors that inspire aggression, facilitate it, and make it a realistic alternative for some. Until we begin asking the right questions, we will continue to spin our wheels."

"Well what do you believe is the cause of violence in the schools?"

"That is a very complicated question. The answer is probably the same for why we have had wars in our entire history as a civilization. Instead of giving you my ideas, because they may not be accurate at all, maybe this is a good question for the staff to get them thinking about it. Simply asking them will help them to feel less powerless and move them away from being victims."

"Can you at least tell me how you see violence happening at this school when there has only been one major instance?"

"Violence to me may be viewed on a continuum. On one end of the continuum would be overt hostility, while closer to the other end would be bullying and then further down would be ridicule and teasing. Every school across the country is dealing with these issues now and unfortunately not as successfully as they would like."

"Why haven't they been successful and how did you know that is going on here?"

Dr. Fanning thought about that for a moment. "As I said, this continuum of violence is potentiated wherever there is a concentration of people who spend a good deal of time together. If this system has a constant source of internal and external pressures, with no process for understanding the effect, there will be more radical results."

To find the entire fictional book, go to www.principalcoach.com or www.teachercoach.com.

This example illustrates just one style of consulting among a vast array of methodology. The Gestalt consultant helps build awareness of existing strengths and limitations, while building energy for change. The trustworthiness of an intervener is measured not by the skills or tools he or she possesses, but by his or her appreciation for how he or she can fit in and relate to the system in which he or she has been called to work. In selecting the right consultant for your school, consider the receptivity of this professional to understanding his or her role in both how he or she perceives him- or herself and how he or she is viewed by others from within.

Once the acceptance level for transformational change is raised to a level where the school is ready to take action, the real work begins. Obstacles of stigmatization and politicking are not eliminated, but they are no longer impediments to moving forward. The next step lies in the creation of a climate that is conducive to self-evaluation, free from fear of recrimination. Get your staff talking to one another in an open and honest way, a way that supports accountability and not blame. Have a staff meeting that does not have an established agenda but is instead an open forum for airing grievances and promoting problem solving. As a school leader you want to facilitate these meetings and not control them. As a teacher you want to bring concerns about the need to be proactive in developing solutions. Everybody needs to be involved from the custodian to the cafeteria staff. Every person who plays a role in a student's life and has an impact on the formation of school culture needs representation.

The creation of a climate conducive to organizational health is a challenging job. As discussed earlier, it may be helpful to bring in a consultant from the outside who can serve as an impartial observer and coach for the growth process. While school leaders and faculty often find the idea of a consultant threatening because they believe they will be told what they are doing wrong, it is helpful to know that qualified consultants build on what is already going well. The helpful consultant will help the faculty find their own strengths and limitations rather than sitting in judgment of the school. A helpful consultant will support the administration while challenging them to become more effective in their leadership role.

For schools with tighter budget constraints it can be helpful to have their staff read the same book or passages from a book such as this. You can even find articles the faculty can read and then discuss during a staff meeting. The idea of development and training needs to be taken seriously, which means that it has to be meaningful and not overly burdensome with regard to time. Teachers typically consider staff development an imposition on their limited time, so they may meet an introduction of change with skepticism. If they know they will become a more integral part of the decision-making process, whether it involves a closer look at policies and procedures (infrastructure) or feedback about the way in which the school is addressing violence prevention (adaptation), they will begin to feel more empowered.

Reducing the potential for violence in your school means a stronger dedication to the improvement of organizational health. There are no quick fixes or magical programs that will stand up to the lack of resiliency and resources our children face every day. No amount of character development can measure up against the temptation of drugs, gangs, and sex. There is no peer mediation program that can withstand the torrent of ostracism and cruelty that children endure when they are at the bottom of a social hierarchy.

The basic impulse to act aggressively in the contex of a culture in which students believe they are alone to face the pressures of fitting in, is more powerful than any punishment for acting out. Zero-tolerance policies should be replaced by extreme-tolerance policies in which we seek to understand inappropriate behavior and how the dynamics of the school play a significant role in modeling acceptable problem solving.

We may never eliminate violence in our society, and that may not even be a realistic goal. But if we can help students learn about dealing with the challenges of life by more effectively addressing the challenges of building a healthy school community, we are doing our jobs.

Glossary

atmosphere. A temporal condition that varies among different groups or subdivisions of the school building and reflects the tone or tension in a specific location.

awareness. The process by which we attend to our internal and external environments. An individual would attend to sensations within the body, while an organization would conceptualize data gained from scanning the internal and external environments.

climate. A specific component of an organizational culture that deals with the mood or milieu of the organization. It is a collection of and interaction by the various moods of individuals within the school. The method by which various systems interrelate to satisfy both the needs of the organization and the individual and also account for the climate of the organization.

contact. For an individual, contact refers to the process of making meaning from what is figural in one's awareness. For an organization it is the overlap of boundaries between subsystems, creating the potential for meaningful exchange across those boundaries.

culture. The invisible fabric of energy that shapes the attitudes, behaviors, and relationships of the faculty and students. Culture is comprised of adaptation, climate, and infrastructure within each organization.

cycle of experience. The process by which individuals and organizations exist, allowing them to make contact across their boundaries. This process also explains the way in which change occurs.

environment. The tangible conditions of the school, such as cleanliness, safety, and physical layout.

infrastructure. The foundation or network of supporting structures responsible for daily operations. The infrastructure is composed of several components, including the mission/vision, philosophical accord, leadership, and shape of the organization.

organizational health. The collective awareness of the internal and external factors that influence the culture of the institution, and use of that awareness toward an active pursuit of improvement in areas identified and agreed upon by the collective membership of the constituents within that system. Such internal and external factors include the three dimensions of culture: adaptation, climate, and infrastructure.

organizational learning. The way in which an organization utilizes information gained from how it manages anticipated and unexpected changes.

resiliency. The tolerance an organization has to internal and external pressure, bending with the change as opposed to resisting it.

resistance. A natural process created by the forces for change and persistence. It occurs on both the individual and group levels.

shape. Status determined by the capabilities of an organization to work toward its goals and how it handles power, control, decision making, leadership, and so forth.

violence. An overt or subtle act of aggression, physical harm, intimidation, or coercion resulting in emotional or physical suffering of another.

Bibliography

American Psychological Association. (1993). *Violence and youth: Psychology's response*. Washington DC: Author.

Astor, R. A., & Meyer, H. A. (2001). The conceptualization of violence-prone schools' subcontexts: Is the sum of the parts greater than the whole? *Urban Education, 36*(3), 374–399.

Astor, R. A., William, J., Kimberly, A., & Wallace, J. M. (1997). Perceptions of school violence as a problem and reports of violent events: A national survey of school social workers. *Social Work, 42*(1), 55–68.

Banathy, B. H. (1992). *A systems view of education: Concepts and principles for effective practice*. Englewood Cliffs, NJ: Educational Technologies Publications.

Benisom, H. (1994). Violence in the workplace. *Training and Development, 48*(1), 26–32.

Bidwell, C. E. (2001). Analyzing schools as organizations: Long-term permanence and short-term change. *Sociology of Education, 74*(2),100–114.

Bluestein, J. (2001). *Creating emotionally safe schools*. Deerfield Beach, FL: Health Communications.

Bower, A. (2001, March 19). Scorecard of hatred. *Time, 157*(11), 31.

Bulach, C. B. (2001). A 4-step process for identifying and reshaping school-culture. *Principal Leadership, 1*(8), 48–51.

Burstyn, J. N., Bender, G., Casella, R., Gordon, H. W., Guerra, D. P., Luschen, K. V, et al. (2001). *Preventing violence in schools: A challenge to American democracy*. Mahwah, NJ: Lawrence Erlbaum.

California Department of Education. (1990, March). *School crime in California for the 1988–89 school year*. (ERIC Document Reproduction Service No. ED 320 225)

Childers, J. H., & Fairman, M. (1986). The school counselor as facilitator of organizational health. *School Counselor, 33*(5), 333–335.

Cloud, J. (2001, March 19). The legacy of Columbine. *Time, 157*(11), 33–35.

Denenberg, T. S., Denenberg, R. V., & Braverman, M. (1998). Reducing violence in U.S. schools. *Dispute Resolution Journal, 53*, 28–35.

DeVoe, J. F., Peter, K., Kaufman, P., Miller, A., Noonan, M., Snyder, T. D., et al. (2004). *Indicators of school crime and safety.* (Report No. NCES 2005-02/NCJ-205290). Washington, DC: U.S. Department of Education.

DiBella, A. J., & Nevis, E. G. (1998). *How organizations learn.* San Francisco: Jossey-Bass.

Dupper, D. R., & Meyer-Adams, N. (2002). Low-level violence: A neglected aspect of school culture. *Urban Education, 37*(3), 350.

Epp, J. R. (1997). *Education and culture: Clinical factors in the formation of character and community in American life. Systemic violence in education: Promise broken.* Albany, NY: SUNY Press.

Everett, S., & Price, J. (1997). Teachers' perception of violence in the public schools. *American Journal of Health, 21*(3), 178–180.

Filippi, S. T. (1996). Violence in the workplace: Containing the problem. *Professional Safety, 41*(6), 37–39.

Finley, L. L. (2002). *Teachers' perception of school safety, safety-based changes, and their resulting impact on school climate: A case study.* Ph.D. dissertation, Western Michigan University, Kalamazoo, MI.

Gabarino, J. (1995). *Raising children in a socially toxic environment.* San Francisco: Jossey-Bass.

Gaustad, J. (1991). Schools respond to gangs and violence. *OSSC Bulletin.* Eugene, OR: Oregon School Study Council.

Glover, D., Cartwright, N., & Gleeson, D. (1998). *Towards bully-free schools: Interventions in action.* Bristol, PA: Open University Press.

Goldstein, N. E., Arnold, D. H., Rosenberg, J. L., Stowe, R. M., & Ortiz, C. (2001). Contagion of aggression in day care classrooms as a function of peer and teacher responses. *Journal of Educational Psychology, 93*(4), 708–719.

Greenbaum, S. (1989). Set straight on bullies. *Journal of National School Safety, 31*, 189.

Hampton, R. L., Jenkins, P., & Gullotta, T. P. (1996). *Preventing violence in America.* Thousand Oaks, CA: Sage

Havemann. J. (1997, February 7) For children, an epidemic of homicide, *Washington Post*, p. A1.

Helms, M. M., & Stern, R. (2001). Exploring the factors that influence employees' perceptions of their organization's culture. *Journal of Management in Medicine, 15*(6), 415–429.

Henry, T. (1994, January 6). Violence in schools grows more severe. *USA Today*, Life Section, p. 1D.

Homes, R. L. (1990). *Nonviolence in theory and in practice*. Belmont, CA: Wadsworth.

Hoy, W. K. (1993). Teachers' sense of efficacy and the organizational health of schools. *Elementary School Journal, 93*(4), 355–372.

Hoy, W. K., & Hannum, J. W. (1997). Middle school climate: An empirical assessment of organizational health and student achievement. *Educational Administration Quarterly, 33*(3), 290–311.

Hoy, W. K., Tarter, C. J., & Bliss, J. R. (1990). Organizational climate, school health, and effectiveness: A comparative analysis. *Educational Administration Quarterly, 26*(3), 260–279.

Ikehara, H. T. (1999). Implications of gestalt theory and practice for the learning organization. *Learning Organization, 6*(2), 63–69.

Janov, J. (1994). *The inventive organization: Hope and daring at work*. San Francisco: Jossey-Bass.

Kaufman, J. (1997). Violence. *Phi Delta Kappa, 79*(4), 320–325.

Kaufman, P., Chen, X., Choy, S. P., Peter, K., Ruddy, S. A., & Miller, A. K. (2001). *Indicators of school crime and safety*. (Report No. NCES 2002-113/NCJ-190775). Washington, DC: U.S. Department of Education.

Kaufman, P., Chen, X., Choy, S. P., Ruddy, S. A., & Miller, A. K. (2001). *Indicators of school crime and safety*. (Report No. NCES 2001-017/NCJ-184176). Washington, DC: U.S. Department of Education.

Keeton, K. B., & Mengistu, B. (1992, Winter). The perception of organizational culture by management level: Implications for training and development. *Public Productivity and Management Review, 16*(2), 205–213.

Licktblau, E. (2001, September 7). FBI urges educators to spot signs of violence. *Los Angeles Times*, pp. 18–22.

Lincoln, Y., & Guba, E. (1995). *Naturalistic inquiry*. Beverly Hills, CA: Sage.

Maguire, K., & Pastore, A. L. (1999). *Sourcebook of criminal statistics, 1998* (U.S. Department of Justice, Office of Justice Programs, Bureau of Justice Statistics, NCJ 176356). Washington, DC: U.S. Government Printing Office.

Markow, D., Fauth, S., & Gravitch, D. (2002). *The Metlife survey of the American teacher*. New York: Metlife.

McCarthy, K. (2000). LIFT violence out of schools. *Psychology Today, 33*, 18–23.

Metlife. (2000). *Key elements of quality schools* (Issue Brief No. 16). New York: Author.

Miles, M. B. (1971). *Administering human resources*. Berkeley, CA: McCutchan.

Mulvey, E. P., & Cauffman, E. (2001). The inherent limits of predicting student violence. *American Psychologist, 56*(10), 797–801.

Napier, A., & Whitaker, C. (1978). *The family crucible*. New York: Harper and Row.

Nevis, E. C. (1987). *Organizational consulting: Gestalt approach*. Cleveland, OH: Gestalt Institute of Cleveland.

O'Leary, K, Griffin, A. M., & Glew, R. W. (1996). Organization-motivated aggression: A research framework. *Academy of Management Review, 21*(1), 225–254.

Organization and Systems Development Center. (1998). *Becoming a better intervener: Theory, concepts, method*. Cambridge, MA: Author.

Osborn, S. M. (1997). *The system made me do it: A life changing approach to organizational politics*. Newark, CA: Life Thread Publications.

Peterson, K. D., & Deal, T. E. (1998). How leaders influence the culture of schools. *Educational Leadership, 56*(1), 28–30.

Pianta, R. C., & Walsh, D. (1996). *High-risk children in the schools: Creating sustaining relationships*. New York: Routledge.

Pietrzak, D., Petersen, G. J., & Speaker, K. M. (1998). Perceptions of school violence by elementary and middle school personnel. *Professional School Counseling, 1*(4), 23–33.

Poole, W. L. (2001). The teacher union's role in 1990's educational reform: An organizational evolution perspective. *Education Administration Quarterly, 37*(2), 173–196.

Price, J. H. (1997). A national assessment of secondary school principals' perceptions of violence in schools. *Health Education and Behavior, 24*(2) 218–229.

Rennison, C., & Rand, M. (2003, August). *Bureau of Justice statistics national crime victimization survey* (Report No. NCJ-199994). Washington, DC: U.S. Department of Justice.

Ritzer, G. (2000). *The McDonaldization of society.* Thousand Oaks, CA: Pine Forge Press.

Sandhu, D. S. (2000). Special issue: School violence and counselors. *Professional School Counseling, 4*(2), iv.

Schein, E. H. (1997). *Organizational culture and leadership.* San Francisco: Jossey-Bass.

Schwartz, W. (1996). *An overview of strategies to reduce school violence* (Report No. 115). New York: Eric Clearinghouse on Urban Education (ERIC Document Reproduction Service No. ED 410321).

Senge, P. (2000). *Schools that learn.* New York: Doubleday.

Shalala, D., & Riley, R. (1994). Joint statement on school health. *Journal of School Health, 64*(4), 135.

Silins, H. C. (1999). What makes a good secondary school? *Journal of Education Administration, 37*(4), 329–339.

Snyder, H. N. (2002). *Juvenile justice bulletin.* Retrieved June 14, 2005, from http://www.ncjrs.org/pdffiles1/ojjdp/204608.pdf.

Srebalus, D. J., Schwartz, J. L., Vaughan, R. V., & Tunick, R. H. (1996). Youth violence in rural schools: Counselor perceptions and treatment resources. *School Counselor, 44*, 1–6.

Stevens, R., & Williams, K. M. (2001). *Preventing violence in schools: A challenge to American democracy.* Mahwah, NJ: Lawrence Erlbaum.

Studner, J. (1996). Understanding and preventing aggressive responses in youth. *Elementary School Guidance and Counseling, 30*, 194–203.

Tucker, N. (2002, April 11). Media report youth violence. *Washington Post,* p. B2.

U.S. Department of Education, National Center for Educational Statistics. (2000, October). *Indicators of school crime and safety* (Report 2001-017/NCJ-184176). Washington, DC: Author.

Walker, D. (1995, March). *School violence prevention* (Report No. 94). Retrieved from http://www.ed.gov/databases/ERIC_Digests/ed379786 .html. (ERIC Document Reproduction Service No. ED 379786)

Warner, B. S., Weist, M. D., & Krulak, A. (1999). Risk factors for school violence. *Urban Education, 34*(1), 52–68.

Williams, W. (1998). Preventing violence in school: What can principals do? *NASSP Bulletin, 82*, 10–17.

About the Author

Jared M. Scherz is the founder of Integrated Training and Consulting (ITC), a multifaceted organization designed to help schools succeed. ITC focuses on school improvement at both the systems and individual levels. An executive coach with over 10 years of experience consulting with school personnel, he is a pioneer in the area of educational transformation.

Before ITC, Jared directed several social service agencies and worked privately as a therapist/coach for managers and other professionals. He earned his bachelor's degree at SUNY Binghamton, his master's degree in education at Penn State University, and his doctorate in clinical psychology at Saybrook University. His dissertation addressed school violence prevention.

He has worked as a school counselor and consultant in various urban and rural schools. From the rural mountains of Pennsylvania to the urban neighborhoods of inner-city Chicago, he has experienced a wide range of problems, including gangs and domestic violence.

On February 29, 2000, a first grader in Flint, Michigan, shot and killed a classmate. This tragic event brought home to Scherz the tremendous need for whole school improvement. He disagreed with the "experts" who came on television to discuss the need for increased prevention efforts. It wasn't their proactive stance that concerned him, but their narrow vision of how to reduce potential student aggression. What seemed to be missing was an appreciation for the school culture—the organizational setting that influences relationships among students and faculty and ultimately sets the school's course toward conflict and peer aggression or toward student learning and school success.

As a result, he changed the course of his professional life. He founded ITC, an organization devoted to the improvement of organizational health in schools. In the years since its inception, he has expanded ITC to include consultation, training, and coaching in a variety of areas related to school culture, focusing specifically on the elimination of student violence. His interest in writing this book is born out of the same desire to help improve the quality of our school systems, both for students and for educators.